GET OFF
THE TOOLS

GET OFF THE TOOLS

The Blueprint to Level up Your Business and Create Freedom

KATIE GODFREY

A&Co.

First published in Great Britain in 2025
by Authors & Co.
www.authorsandco.pub

Copyright © Katie Godfrey 2025

Katie Godfrey asserts the moral right to be identified as the author
of this work in accordance with the Copyright, Designs and
Patents Act 1988.

ISBN 978-1-917623-07-0 (paperback)
ISBN 978-1-917623-08-7 (hardback)

Disclaimer
The information provided in this book is for educational and
informational purposes only. It is not intended to be, and should
not be considered, financial advice. All efforts have been made to
ensure the accuracy of the information contained herein; however,
the author and publisher make no representations or warranties
regarding the completeness, accuracy, or timeliness of any
information. The reader should consult with a qualified financial
professional before making any financial decisions.

To all the girls out there who were told they wouldn't become anything. Remember, you can be whatever you dream of being. You just have to act on that dream.

To my children, Lola-Rose and Brodee. I love you more than I could ever explain. Thank you for being the driving force behind everything I do. It's all for you.

To my parents, thank you for supporting my young dream when most wouldn't have. Mum, you're my biggest supporter and my listening ear always. I will never be able to thank you enough for everything you have done and continue to do. I'm so lucky to call you my mum.

To my fiancé, Luke, thank you for putting up with me and my crazy ideas, for being by my side always and being the best father to our children. I love you.

CONTENTS

1

FREEDOM AND GETTING FULLY BOOKED

How do you gain clients and get fully booked? This is the question I hear every day. You started this salon or clinic business for flexibility and freedom, but you feel completely trapped, with the business running *you*. You post on social media all the time, but it's crickets; clients don't even like or comment on your hard work. Are they even seeing your posts?

I hear these problems every day. Over the years, I've learned many lessons about how to run a successful business. One of them is that you need so much more than social media. This book will teach you many steps in an easy-to-follow way that will help you get fully booked, get off the tools and find the freedom you've always wanted.

When I opened the doors to my shiny, brand-new salon, I couldn't believe it was all mine. I had had my eyes on this building for a while and now I was here – just me. All I had to do (!) was get clients through the door to pay the overheads and deal with the £50,000 of debt I had incurred.

It turned out to be a lot harder than I thought it would be. Drowning in debt, I kept investing in the latest trends as they came out, thinking clients would flock in because we offered the newest treatments. If only! It definitely didn't work out that way.

I wouldn't recommend anyone set up a salon or clinic with zero client base and zero experience. It was slightly crazy. I had no qualifications in business; I didn't even finish school, having left at thirteen years old because of bullying. I had no previous experience doing beauty treatments and no clientele built before I opened the doors.

If a client came to me now and said they were going to do what I did, I would recommend a strong *no…* don't do it this way. Build the business first. Work from home or rent space. Once you have clientele then go and get a salon. I want to help you get to your idea of success, without repeating my mistakes.

I always go against the rules. My mum always said to me when I was growing up, "I could never put you in a box." I do not want to put you in a box either. We all must go on our own journeys and do what feels right to us. But I do sometimes wish I had done things differently back then. Maybe if I hadn't gone against all the rules, the journey might not have been as hard! At the same time, it has definitely formed me as a businesswoman.

I didn't know how to market a business, how to grow it or how to get clients to book in, let alone understand client experiences and customer service. But what I did have was a lot of determination, focus, and a desire for a successful business. I was ready to soak up anything I could learn to prove those bullies wrong and show that I could be something, even though they had wrecked my childhood. That wasn't going to define me.

My journey wasn't easy. I remember the sleepless nights, the endless worries about bills, and the constant fear of failure. There were days I questioned my sanity, wondering if I had made a terrible mistake. But every time doubt crept in, I reminded myself why I started. I wanted to create something beautiful, something that was mine, and something that could provide for me not just for now but for my future.

What is your reason for building your business? In other words, what is your 'why'? It could be anything, so long as it motivates you. Perhaps it is your children, or proving a parent wrong, or maybe even leaving behind the upbringing you had. It can be anything that's personal to you. Mine was definitely proving bullies wrong and showing myself that I could do something even without grades. It is always good to have your 'why' clear in your mind, so you can keep focused during the hard times.

Since starting my salon and building other companies, I can proudly say that I now have qualifications under my belt. I have grown into a qualified business strategist, life coach and educator. These achievements didn't come overnight. They are the result of years of hard work, late nights, and wanting to help my clients even more than I could before. I attended every seminar I could find, read countless books, listened to podcasts, took on the best mentors and have been part of top masterminds to make sure I'm always learning and growing. Education really doesn't stop. It is funny that I should say that, seeing as I hated the school system so much. Being dyslexic was a battle. Yes, I am dyslexic, and now I'm writing this book. If I can teach you anything at all, it is that you can do anything you set your mind to.

Over the years, I've learned how to build a business, maintain the mindset needed to keep going, become a number one brand, and run successful businesses that operate without me. I have had a chain of salons, training academies across the country and a product range sold worldwide. Each venture taught me invaluable lessons about resilience, innovation and the importance of building a strong team. It is now my passion to help and support you to do the same.

You want your business to give you freedom. What's the point of starting a business if it's going to run *you*? If you become a slave to your business and clients, it only leads to burnout and resentment. Maybe you even feel that right now. If you do, that can change. I can speed up your path to success, fast-forwarding you, skipping all the mistakes I made and teaching you exactly what I did well.

This book will make you fall in love with your business and get excited to work *on* it rather than *in* it. It will give you clear direction on how to grow your business, turn your clients into raving fans and ultimately make more money. Imagine waking up every day with a sense of purpose and excitement, knowing your business is thriving and you have the freedom to live life on your terms.

Many of you went into business because you're great at the service. Maybe you worked for someone, had a strong client base, and decided to set up on your own. Or maybe you have always worked for yourself but have grown and got yourself a salon or clinic. Regardless of someone's situation, the most common thing I hear from people who ask for my help is that they're great at the service but have no idea about 'business'.

I promise you, after reading this book, you will have full insights on how to run a real business. We'll cover everything from business foundations to marketing strategies for scaling your beauty business. You'll learn how to attract and retain clients, manage your finances and create a brand that stands out in a crowded market. You can stop winging it.

You are running a business even though you probably call it your *job*. Learning these things is crucial. You wouldn't become a doctor without studying to be one or a train driver without the training. Learning and understanding business is exactly the same. You must be invested and learn how to nurture and grow it. I have been in the hair, beauty, and aesthetics industry for so many years it's in my blood. But I am highly passionate about business in general. The principles of running a successful business are universal, and the insights in this book are applicable regardless of your field.

The real turning point for me came when I found out I was pregnant. I had two salons, a training academy and a product range. Not only that, I was single. How could I keep these businesses going and have this baby on my own when all the clients wanted me and I was the biggest earner? I had to work differently. I had to create freedom in business, gain teams, and make the companies run like clockwork.

Having my daughter single-handedly was the best thing that could have happened to my business. We have been able to travel the world while still earning, giving her (and now my son) the life I dreamed of. I have also helped my clients do the same, having families yet still running their businesses around their lifestyles.

Take, for example, my client, Ebonie, from Ebonie Blush. It was just her, working every hour God sent, and she hired me as her coach because she wanted to grow her salon and build a team. Soon after, she discovered she was pregnant. Now, not only did she need to learn to be a manager, leader and marketer, but to get to the point where the salon ran completely without her.

Within twelve months, she had three staff members and was off the salon floor. It was definitely a testing time for Ebonie, but she was able to have her baby without worrying about losing her business. Fast forward to now, her salon is doing incredibly well, she gets to have time with her baby girl and takes holidays while the business makes money. Who says women can't do both?

I have worked with countless other entrepreneurs facing similar challenges. I remember 'Sarah', a talented aesthetic practitioner overwhelmed with the demands of running her clinic. She was constantly putting out fires and had no time to focus on growth. We set up systems that streamlined the day-to-day business, freed up her time and allowed her to focus on what she loved most: serving her clients. Today, Sarah's clinic is one of the most sought-after in her area, and she has a team of dedicated professionals who share her vision.

Let's get started on building *your* business. In each chapter, you will learn something new to bring into your world. See this book as a step-by-step business guide. Learn about marketing your business, taking on a team, managing your time and managing your mindset regarding your money and your daily life. They are all crucial for riding the roller coaster of business.

It isn't just about making money; it's about creating a life you love. You will also read about setting boundaries, prioritising self-care, and finding a balance that suits you.

Whether you're just starting out or looking to take your established business to the next level, this book is your roadmap to success. You don't have to do this alone. I am with you every step of the way, cheering you on and sharing the lessons I've learned. Together, we can build your business so that it not only thrives but gives you the freedom and fulfilment you deserve.

Katie and her daughter Lola-Rose.
Traveling together as a single mum.

2

THE HEART OF YOUR BUSINESS...
KNOWING YOUR IDEAL CLIENT

Building a successful beauty business is about more than offering exceptional services. It is about attracting the right clients, that is, those who resonate with your brand, appreciate your treatments and services, and want to pay for what you offer. This begins with identifying and understanding your ideal client. Knowing your ideal client could very well be the difference between a business that thrives and one that just about survives. Many of us completely forget to do this and try to cater for everyone out there, gaining every client we possibly can. If you try to talk to everyone, you talk to no one.

When you first started your business, you likely had a vision of who you wanted to serve. You probably knew which clients you wanted to spend time with day in, day out. Perhaps you imagined your ideal client as someone who loves luxury, values self-care and seeks out the best in beauty services. Or maybe your focus was on someone who values efficiency, results and the best aesthetic treatments. Whatever your vision, identifying your ideal client is not just a nice-to-have, it's essential.

In the rush to get clients through the door, it can be tempting to try to be everything to everyone. You might find yourself chasing any client who shows interest, whether or not they truly align with your brand or if you want to serve them. This scattergun approach leads to frustration, burnout, and, worst of all, a diluted brand that fails to stand out in a crowded market.

The purpose of this chapter is to guide you through the process of identifying your ideal client. You will get to know the person or group of people who will not only appreciate what you offer but will become loyal, raving fans of your business. You will understand why it's crucial to define this client clearly and how doing so can transform your business, making it more profitable and more enjoyable.

Understanding your ideal client isn't only about demographics like age, gender or location. It means digging deeper to understand their needs, desires and pain points, knowing what keeps them up at night and how your services can solve their problems or enhance their lives. When you have a clear picture of your ideal client, every decision you make, from marketing strategies to service offerings, becomes more focused and effective. Having that one person in mind is truly powerful.

Throughout this chapter, you'll learn how to identify your ideal client, understand their motivations, and tailor your business to meet their needs. We'll look at practical steps to define this client profile and to attract and retain the people who are the best fit for your business.

By the end of this chapter, you'll have a deeper understanding of why knowing your ideal client is the foundation of a successful beauty business and how you can apply this knowledge to create a business that not only grows but also gives you the freedom and financial rewards you've always dreamed of.

THE BLUEPRINT FOR CREATING A CONCEPT FOR YOUR IDEAL CLIENT

In the beauty, hair and aesthetics industry, competition is fierce and trends are ever-changing. In such a world, the concept of the "ideal client" might seem obvious and unnecessary – you may even think boring – but there are many layers to it, and these layers can strongly influence the direction of your business. So, what exactly is an ideal client, and why is it so crucial to define them?

An ideal client is more than someone who walks through your door and is willing to pay for your services. They are the perfect fit for your business in every sense. They value what you offer, resonate with your brand's ethos, and are likely to become repeat clients for your business. Essentially, they are the clients who appreciate your services and are willing to pay a premium for the experience you provide.

Not all clients are the same. While it's tempting to think that every paying client is a good client, this isn't necessarily the case. Some clients might demand excessive time and energy, create stress for your team, or simply not align with the values and standards you set for your business. On the other hand, your *ideal* clients make your work rewarding, both emotionally and financially.

They have specific needs and desires that align with what you offer, and they see the value in your services, which makes them more likely to be loyal, long-term clients. This is what you want: it means you can think about the lifetime value of a client rather than the value of a single treatment. That client will come to you many times over a long period. They also tend to be more understanding, respectful, and appreciative of you and your business. In other words, your ideal client is someone who perfectly matches your services, pricing, and business philosophy. We all have those clients we dread calling for an appointment and we tell them we are fully booked to try and steer them away. Or that client that books online and we pray they will cancel their appointment. These are not your ideal clients.

Everything about running your business becomes more focused and effective when you have a clear picture of your ideal client. Your marketing messages become clearer and more targeted, attracting more of the right people. Your services can be tailored to meet the specific needs of this client, making sure that you provide exactly what they are looking for. This match between what you offer and what your ideal client needs leads to more client satisfaction, more referrals, and ultimately, more revenue.

Imagine running a beauty business where every client feels like a perfect match. Every time you open the diary you are excited about who is in next. They appreciate your services, respect your pricing and your policies and spread the word about your business. This is the reality you can create when you focus on serving your ideal clients and not 'female, aged sixteen to eighty' which is what I hear all the time when I ask a salon or clinic who their ideal client is. When you try to appeal to everyone, you often end up diluting your brand and attracting clients who don't fully appreciate your business. This can lead to frustration, lower profits, and dreading going to work.

Business owners often have several misconceptions about the idea of the ideal client, and it's important to address these upfront. One of the most common myths is that narrowing your focus to a specific client type will limit your appointment bookings. In reality, the opposite is true. By honing your ideal client profile, you actually create more opportunities for your business to grow and get fully booked.

Another misconception is the belief that defining an ideal client is a one-time task. Your ideal client profile may change as your business grows and as trends shift in the beauty industry. It needs regular check-ins to ensure you're always in tune with the needs and desires of your most valued clients. I tend to find our ideal clients are a past version of us. Then as we grow and evolve, so does our ideal client. For example, when I first started my salon, we focused on tanning and nails. I loved these two treatments and it's actually embarrassing how much I used to tan. My ideal client was exactly the same as me. As I grew older, my skin became more of a focus, and I found myself wanting to push more of these types of treatments – which meant my ideal client needed to change too.

Some business owners also fear that by focusing on an ideal client, they might alienate other potential clients. While it's true that a more defined focus might mean saying no to certain types of clients, this strategic decision frees up your time and energy to focus on those who truly align with your brand. These ideal clients are the ones who will drive your business forward, not only through their loyalty and spending but also through the positive word-of-mouth they generate.

Finally, there's the misconception that identifying an ideal client is only about demographics like age, gender or location. While these factors are important, they're just the beginning. A true ideal client profile goes much deeper, incorporating psychographics such as values, lifestyle and personality traits, and understanding their specific needs, challenges and desires. This view of your ideal client allows you to connect with them on a deeper level through your marketing and make sure that your business stands out to them.

THE POWER OF IDENTIFYING YOUR PERFECT CLIENT

Identifying your ideal client is one of the most powerful steps you can take to ensure the success of your beauty business. When you know exactly who your ideal client is, you can tailor your services, marketing and overall business strategy to meet their needs and wants. This focused approach not only helps you attract more of the right clients but also leads to greater satisfaction for you and your customers. Let's explore the key benefits of knowing your ideal client and how it can transform your business.

TARGETED MARKETING

One of the biggest advantages of knowing your ideal client is how much easier it makes it to work on your marketing strategy. Instead of trying to reach everyone, you can focus your efforts on attracting that one type of person most likely to be interested in your services. This means your marketing messages can be more specific and relevant, which increases the chances of resonating with your audience.

For example, if your ideal client is a woman in her thirties who is passionate about skincare and prefers natural products, you can craft your marketing messages to speak directly to her needs and preferences. Your social media posts, website content and advertisements can all reflect the values and needs of this client, making it more likely that she will choose your business over a competitor's.

This not only saves you time and money, but makes your marketing efforts more effective. When your messaging is clear and focused, it attracts the right people and encourages them to take action, whether that's booking an appointment, signing up for your regular emails, or following you on social media.

INCREASED CLIENT SATISFACTION

Another huge benefit of knowing who your ideal client is, is that it leads to higher client satisfaction. When you understand their needs and preferences, you can tailor your services to meet their expectations. This personalised approach makes clients feel valued and understood, which in turn increases their satisfaction with your treatments.

For instance, if your ideal client values a luxurious, relaxing experience, you can design your services and environment to create that feeling of indulgence. From the moment they walk into your salon or clinic, they should feel like they are being pampered in a way that aligns with their desires. When clients feel that you understand them and are catering to their needs, they are more likely to become repeat clients and recommend your salon to others.

Happy clients are also more likely to leave positive reviews and testimonials, which can attract even more of your ideal clients. In this way, understanding your ideal client creates a positive cycle of satisfaction, loyalty and growth.

BETTER BUSINESS DECISIONS

Knowing your ideal client also helps you to make better business decisions. When you have a clear picture of whom you're serving, you can make informed choices about everything from the services you offer to the way you price them. Your ideal client profile can guide you in developing new products, expanding your service menu, and even deciding on the décor and ambience of your salon.

For example, if your ideal client values high-end, luxury services, you might decide to invest in premium products and create a more upscale environment. On the other hand, if your ideal client is budget-conscious but still wants quality services, you might focus on offering affordable packages or discounts.

A well-defined ideal client also helps you determine where to allocate your resources. Instead of spending money on marketing campaigns that might not reach the right people, you can invest in strategies that are more likely to attract your ideal clients. This focused approach leads to better use of your time, energy and money, making your business more efficient and profitable.

EFFICIENCY IN RESOURCES

Focusing on your ideal client allows you to use your resources of time, money and effort, more efficiently. When you know who you're targeting, you can streamline your operations to better serve these clients. This might mean training your staff to specialise in certain services, investing in certain products, or even adjusting your business hours to accommodate your ideal client's schedule.

For example, if your ideal client is a busy professional who prefers evening appointments, you might decide to extend your hours on certain days to cater to this demand. By aligning your business with the needs of your ideal client, you provide the best possible service while maximising your resources.

Focusing on your ideal client reduces the risk of burnout. When you try to please everyone, it's easy to spread yourself too thin and become overwhelmed. When you concentrate on serving a specific group of clients, you can manage your workload more effectively and create a business that is sustainable in the long term.

Identifying your ideal client brings many benefits that can hugely impact the success and growth of your beauty business. From more effective marketing to increased client spend, better business decisions and more efficient use of resources, knowing your ideal client allows you to build a business that is both profitable and fulfilling. By focusing on the people who truly appreciate and value what you offer, you create a strong foundation for long-term success.

STEPS TO DISCOVERING YOUR PERFECT CLIENT

Figuring out your ideal, perfect client is one of the main steps in building a successful beauty business. It allows you to tailor your services, marketing efforts and overall strategy to attract the clients who will benefit most from what you offer. In this section, you will find a step-by-step approach to identify *your* ideal client, and then make sure that every aspect of your business aligns with their needs, wants and desires.

STEP 1

Start by looking at your existing client base, because your current clients can show you who your ideal clients might be. Begin by analysing the clients who are already loyal to your business. Who are the clients that book regularly, refer others, provide positive feedback, and you love working with? These clients are likely to give you a good picture of your ideal client. List these clients' names.

To get a clearer picture, consider the following questions:

- What characteristics do your best clients have in common?
- What services do they typically book?
- How often do they visit?
- What do they value most about your business?
- What do they have in common in terms of age, occupation, lifestyle and spending habits?

By getting this information together, you can start to see patterns that will help you define your ideal client. Pay particular attention to the clients who bring you the most happiness and satisfaction. You know those clients you're excited to see when you open up that diary for the day? These are the people you should aim to attract more of.

STEP 2

Once you've looked at your current clients, the next step is to create a detailed client persona. A client persona is a representation of your ideal client based on the data you've gathered. Creating this persona helps you to visualise who you are trying to reach and makes it easier to tailor your marketing and services to their needs.

To create a client persona, start by giving them a name and basic demographic details, such as age, gender, occupation and income level. Then, dive deeper into their lifestyle, values and behaviours. Consider questions like:

- What are their main concerns or pain points when it comes to beauty and self-care?
- What motivates them to book services at a beauty salon or clinic?

- What are their favourite products or treatments?
- How do they spend their free time?
- What social media platforms do they use?
- What kind of experience do they want when they visit your business?
- What TV programmes do they like to watch?
- How many times a year do they go on holiday?

For example, you might create a persona like this:

- Name: Sarah
- Age: 35
- Occupation: Marketing Director
- Income: £60,000 per year
- Lifestyle: Busy professional with little free time; values self-care and high-quality products; enjoys luxury experiences, frequently uses Instagram and Pinterest for beauty inspiration.
- Pain Points: Needs quick, high-quality services that fit into her busy schedule; prefers organic and cruelty-free products.
- Motivation: Wants to look polished and feel confident without spending too much time on her beauty routine.

By creating a detailed persona like Sarah, you can better understand your ideal clients' needs and how to attract them to your business.

STEP 3

In addition to analysing your current clients, it's a must to look at market research on a broader scale to gather more information about your potential clients. This step involves understanding the larger market trends, as well as the particular needs and wants of the clients you want to attract.

There are several ways to gather this information:

- Surveys and Questionnaires: Send out surveys to your current clients asking about their preferences, needs and experiences. Include questions that will help you understand their motivations and challenges. You could even hold a twenty-minute focus group with your top clients to gather this information.
- Social Media Analysis: Use tools like Instagram Insights or Facebook Analytics to see who engages with your content. What are their demographics? What types of posts do they interact with most?
- Competitor Research: Look at the clients your competitors attract. What can you learn from their client base to help you refine your own ideal client profile? Don't go down a rabbit hole here looking at competitors: it is strictly research, not a copying exercise.

The more information you collect, the more accurate and useful your ideal client profile (or persona) will be.

STEP 4

To really connect with your ideal clients, you need to understand what drives them. What are their deepest desires and motivations when it comes to beauty and self-care? Understanding these motivations will allow you to speak directly to them in your marketing.

Consider the following:

- Emotional Needs: What emotional benefits do your clients want? Are they looking for confidence, relaxation, rejuvenation or perhaps a sense of luxury?
- Functional Needs: What practical problems are they trying to solve? Are they looking for quick services that fit into their busy schedules or do they want specialised treatments for skin or hair concerns?
- Values: What values do your clients hold? Do they prioritise sustainability, vegan products or high-end luxury experiences?

By understanding these motivations, you can create a client experience that resonates with your ideal clients on a deeper level, making them more likely to choose your business over others.

STEP 5

Finding your ideal client is not a one-time task. As your business grows and evolves – just as you grow and evolve as a person – so too might your ideal client profile. It is important to review and refine your client personas regularly to make sure they remain accurate and relevant.

Test and perfect your ideal client profile in these ways:

- Marketing Campaigns: Try different marketing messages or offers targeted at different segments of your ideal client profile. See which ones resonate the most and play around to see what works.
- Client Feedback: Always gather feedback and reviews from your clients to make sure their needs are being met. Use this feedback to narrow down your understanding of who your ideal client is.

- Monitor Trends: Stay informed about industry trends and how they might affect your ideal client. For example, if there's a growing trend toward natural and organic products, this might shift the preferences of your ideal client.

By regularly refining and testing your ideal client profile, you can make sure your salon stays aligned with the clients who matter most.

By analysing your current clients, creating a detailed client persona, gathering data, understanding client motivations, and continually refining your profile, you can build a clear picture of the people who are most likely to appreciate and support your business. This helps you make better decisions, create more effective marketing strategies, and ultimately attract more of the clients you love to work with.

Understanding your ideal client is great, but seeing how it works in real-world scenarios can make the concept even more powerful. Let me introduce you to my client Alice Widdows, the owner of Wynyard Therapy in the Northeast. She had been in the yachting industry for twenty-five years, organising very high-end luxury events. In 2022, Alice bought an existing salon with the vision of bringing high-end luxury into the beauty space. It had been going for twelve years as a hair and beauty salon. The salon had a clientele but offered very low-priced treatments and there was no experience attached. It was very different from the salon Alice envisioned as a beauty and wellness destination.

The first thing Alice had to work on when she took over the salon was her ideal client. She needed to tweak the services being offered, increase her pricing and change the whole customer experience to work towards her vision for the business. We both knew she would lose clients as they weren't the ideal client for the type of business she was trying to create. Alice had to create a new client avatar for her salon, which was a version of herself, and be ok with losing clients to gain new ones.

It was definitely a hard journey; she needed a lot of determination and to keep the end goal in mind. But with new marketing, messaging, premium products, team training and technology, Alice changed this business around. She also launched a membership subscription. Within a year of hard work and change, the business has gone from £8,000 months to over £23,000 months. Can you imagine nearly tripling your turnover?

HOW TO GROW AS YOUR CLIENTS CHANGE

Identifying your ideal client is not a one-time task. Your ideal client in a few years might not be the same as your ideal client today. It is an ongoing process that evolves as you, your business and the market change.

The beauty industry is constantly evolving. New trends come in all the time, client preferences shift, and the needs of your target market may change. As these changes happen, what was once relevant to your clients might no longer resonate, and long-term success depends on staying attuned to these changes. You must adapt and evolve with your ideal client to ensure your business continues to grow through these changes.

Consider how beauty trends have changed over the past decade. Clients who once preferred traditional beauty treatments might now be interested in more aesthetic treatments or advanced treatments. If your business doesn't adapt to these changing preferences, you risk losing relevance and connection with your ideal clients.

My salon used to be huge on tanning. We offered sunbeds and spray tans. Over the years we saw that my ideal client didn't want tanning anymore. As they grew older with the salon, they became more into skincare and anti-ageing, which didn't align with our sunbeds. We sold one and kept one, which meant we had more space for new treatments.

With spray tans, we used to have a young ideal client. They loved a tan on a Thursday or Friday night. Again, as the ideal client changed, so did this trend. We still took bookings for spray tans but made the decision in the end to stop doing tans altogether. We still had clients who wanted them, but when we weighed up the number of other treatments we had to turn away due to what our ideal clients wanted, we made more money by removing the tanning space and using it for more popular treatments.

One of the best ways to make sure you evolve with your ideal client is to stay informed about industry trends and client preferences. You can do this in many ways:

Regular Feedback: Continuously ask for feedback from your clients. Use surveys, comment cards or informal conversations to gauge their satisfaction and interest in new services and experiences. This feedback will provide valuable insights into how their needs are changing.

Market Research: Keep an eye on broader industry trends. Follow beauty industry news, attend trade shows and events, and take part in professional networks to stay ahead of upcoming trends. This will help you see changes in your ideal client's preferences and adjust your services accordingly.

Social Media Monitoring: Social media platforms are a goldmine for understanding what currently interests your clients. Monitor hashtags, follow influencers in the beauty industry, and pay attention to what your clients share and engage with online.

As you gather new information about your clients, be prepared to adapt your business strategy to serve them more. This might involve updating your treatments, changing your marketing, or even rebranding your business to better align with your evolving ideal client profile.

For example, if you notice a growing interest in organic beauty products, you might consider expanding your product line to include more eco-friendly options. If your ideal client demographic shifts from young clients to more mature clients, you might need to adjust your marketing messages and treatments to suit their needs, as I did.

Making changes ensures your business stays relevant and continues to attract your ideal clients. It also shows you are responsive to their needs, which builds that all-important trust and loyalty.

Flexibility is key when it comes to evolving with your ideal client. You don't want to stand still or be known as the old-school salon. The businesses that carry on growing and stick around long term are those that pivot and adapt to changes in the market and the world. You don't have to completely overhaul your business every time something new comes out. It is about being open to change and willing to make adjustments that keep your business aligned with the needs of your clients.

A flexible approach keeps you ahead of the curve and ensures your business continues to meet the demands of your clients. It helps you retain existing clients and attract new ones looking for a business that understands and caters to their needs.

3

MARKETING GENIUS

I think marketing might be my favourite subject. There is so much involved and so much to go over that I could write a whole book just on marketing. But I won't. I can't stand books where you're waiting for some answers, reading, reading and there are no answers! I will give you the top things to do within your business straight away that will make a huge difference. Are you ready?

When people think of marketing, they mainly think of social media. That's it. But this is where a lot of hair, beauty and aesthetic businesses go wrong. Yes, we definitely need social media platforms. In fact, they are non-negotiable. But don't put all your eggs in one basket, even more so on platforms where you don't own the data.

We have all been there at a time when Instagram went down. There was a time not so long ago when the whole of Meta went down: Instagram, Facebook and WhatsApp. So many people freaked out, including myself. First of all, I thought I had been hacked when I couldn't get into my accounts, but not long after that, my whole network panicked because the platforms were down. They soon bounced back, but let's just think for a minute. If social media went down tomorrow, gone, didn't come back... what would happen to your business? How would you get new clients? How would you promote new treatments?

I bet you are thinking now, *no idea!* You would be screwed and have no business left. Remember that you don't own that data. Yes, you need to build a following and social media will be a big way you get new clients through the door, but you don't want it to be your lifeline or your only strategy to getting new clients.

The data you do own is an e-mail list. I can't believe how many people still don't use email marketing. It is mad. You are missing a huge trick if you're not currently doing this in your business. It helps you gain new bookings, gets existing clients to return faster, increases a client's spend and gets past clients who haven't been back in a while to rebook. So why would you not do it? Add this to your to-do list immediately.

The comebacks I hear about email marketing are as follows: Everyone gets hundreds of emails a day so they aren't going to see mine. No one wants to hear from me and I have no idea what to even write. People don't want to be sold to all the time.

Let's break this down. Yes, we all get a lot of e-mail a day, but companies do this because it works. The more you're in someone's inbox, the more you get seen and the more sales you will make.

Think about how you manage your own emails. Most of us have the mail app on our phones. Many of us have a notification that pings when an email comes through, which alerts us to check who it is from. If we don't have notifications switched on, we often check our inbox a few times a day. When you open your inbox, you normally decide which message to open because of the subject line.

If you are doing e-mail marketing now but not making sales, test different subject lines.

You can have the best-written email, the most irresistible offer, but if that subject line isn't clickbait, no one is even getting to the email. Think about the subject lines that make you open an email. Perhaps something that has your name in it works well.

Email marketing systems are so clever nowadays that you can see how many people open your email on the insights. If you currently send marketing emails, look at which emails have the highest open rate. Then play around with similar subject lines.

If people don't want to hear from you, they will unsubscribe. If they do want to hear from you, they will open the email when they are ready. I speak to so many people who worry about the unsubscribes and even about the unfollows on social media.

I wouldn't worry about those things. In fact, I would go further and say not to even look at those stats. If someone unsubscribes or unfollows, look at this as a good thing as they are not your ideal client. You haven't pissed them off with too many emails; they just aren't your ideal client and, in fact, you don't want them on your list because they will never buy. Email systems normally cost, too. As your list grows, you pay more money to the provider, so let unsubscribers go without worrying.

Let's talk about those numbers. The number of followers you have and the number of people on your email list do matter – but only if they are your perfect ideal clients. Some of my clients have had incredible launches with only three hundred followers. I know of others who haven't done as well, with ten thousand followers. This is completely down to the followers not being ideal clients. Maybe you have lots of friends, family and other people following you, but not necessarily those who would buy from you. Generating sales and gaining appointments is a numbers game. The more ideal clients you have following you, the more sales you will make.

This is why part of my strategy in each of my businesses is to get in front of lots of people every single day and gain more leads. I currently have an audience of over eighty thousand people across socials and emails. But I know that if I can connect with more of my ideal clients and keep growing my email list, I will make even more sales when I launch something new or when I have space available.

Only around five percent of your social media posts will be seen and only around twenty percent of your emails will be opened. The more you grow your audience, the more people that five percent will reach or the more people will be in that twenty percent who open that email. This is why marketing is so important!

Let's move on to the myth that people don't want to be sold to. I would say you're right that people don't want to be sold to all the time, but you still need to sell. It is a balancing act. You are in business and that means you need to sell every day in some shape or form. If you don't sell, who is going to know who you are? Who will urge people to get those appointments booked? No one will sell your services and business like you. You just don't realise you're already doing it daily.

If you sold all the time in your content, people would switch off. If you put all motivational content out there, people will get bored after a while. When you create emails, you need to make sure you add sales in there, but also educational, motivational and trust content, exactly the same as your social media posts. Balancing the four pillars of sales, educational content, motivational content and trust will work wonders. A mix of these types of content gets your potential clients to like, know and trust your business before they say yes to buying. It also helps you decide what to write in your emails and your social media content as you have a guide to work with. Keep rotating each pillar and that will help.

Let me help you get some ideas of what you could write about for each pillar.

EDUCATIONAL CONTENT:

1. Treatment Tips:
   – Daily treatment care routines.
   – Tips for maintaining different treatments.
   – How to protect your hair, lashes, nails, etc.

2. Advice:
   – Steps for an effective routine.
   – Tips for different skin types/hair types.
   – Importance of SPF and how to use it correctly.

3. Tutorials:
   – Step-by-step guides for different looks.
   – Tips for applying products.
   – Seasonal trends.

4. Product Recommendations:
   – Reviews of popular products.
   – Demonstrations of how to use specific products.
   – Comparison of products for different needs.

5. Before and After Transformations:
  – Showcasing client transformations.
  – Highlighting different services.

6. DIY Beauty Treatments:
  – Home remedies for hair and skin.
  – Simple DIY masks and treatments.
  – Benefits and cautions of DIY beauty.

7. Behind-the-Scenes Content:
  – A day in the life at the salon.
  – Meet the team and their specialities.
  – Tour of the salon and facilities.

8. Client Testimonials and Stories:
  – Featuring happy clients.
  – Sharing success stories and feedback.
  – Encouraging clients to share their own stories.

9. Beauty/Hair Industry News and Trends:
  – Latest trends in hair and beauty.
  – New products and technologies.
  – Insights from conferences and events.

10. Interactive Content:
  – Q&A sessions with stylists and beauty experts.
  – Polls and surveys about beauty preferences.
  – Live demonstrations and tutorials.

11. Health and Wellness Tips:
  - Nutrition tips for healthy hair and skin.
  - Importance of hydration.
  - Relaxation techniques and stress management.

12. Seasonal Beauty Tips:
  - Adjusting routines for different seasons.
  - Special care tips for summer and winter.
  - Seasonal makeup and hair trends.

13. Hair and Skin Myths Debunked:
  - Common misconceptions about hair and skincare.
  - Facts versus myths segments.
  - Scientific explanations behind popular beliefs.

14. Event Promotions and Specials:
  - Announcing upcoming events and promotions.
  - Special deals and discounts.
  - Exclusive offers for social media followers.

15. Collaborations and Guest Posts:
  - Collaborating with influencers and other beauty/hair professionals.
  - Guest posts and takeovers by experts.
  - Joint live sessions with other businesses.

SALES CONTENT:

1. Service Highlights:
    – Detailed descriptions of services offered (haircuts, colouring, facials, etc.).
    – Benefits and features of each service.
    – Special packages or bundles.

2. Promotional Offers:
    – Announcements of current promotions and discounts.
    – Limited-time offers and flash sales.
    – Holiday and seasonal specials.

3. Product Promotions:
    – Highlighting new arrivals in products.
    – Exclusive products available only at the salon.
    – Product bundles and gift sets.

4. Membership and Loyalty Programmes:
    – Details about loyalty rewards programmes.
    – Benefits of joining membership programmes.
    – Special offers for members.

5. Gift Certificates:
    – Promotion of gift certificates for special occasions.
    – Special packages for holidays and events.
    – Incentives for purchasing gift certificates.

6. Referral Programmes:
  - Encouraging clients to refer friends and family.
  - Rewards and discounts for successful referrals.
  - Sharing referral success stories.

7. Client Appreciation Events:
  - Invitations to exclusive client appreciation events.
  - Special deals available only at these events.
  - Showcasing event highlights and client experiences.

8. Exclusive Social Media Offers:
  - Special discounts for social media followers.
  - Promo codes and coupons shared on social media.
  - Contests and giveaways for followers.

9. Seasonal Service Packages:
  - Bundled services tailored for different seasons.
  - Holiday-themed packages (e.g., Valentine's Day, Christmas).
  - Promotions for back-to-school, summer, etc.

10. New Service Launches:
  - Announcing the introduction of new services.
  - Introductory discounts and offers for new services.
  - Behind-the-scenes look at new service preparations.

11. Limited-Time Service Upgrades:
    – Offering complementary or discounted upgrades.
    – Promoting add-ons like deep conditioning, scalp treatments, hand massage, etc.
    – Special deals on premium services.

12. Client Success Stories:
    – Featuring testimonials and reviews from satisfied clients.
    – Before and after photos showcasing transformations.
    – Personal stories about the positive impact of salon services.

13. Event Partnerships:
    – Collaborating with local events for special promotions.
    – Cross-promotions with other businesses.
    – Highlighting joint events and special offers.

14. Interactive Sales Campaigns:
    – Hosting live sales events on social media.
    – Interactive Q&A sessions about services and products.
    – Polls and surveys to engage followers and offer deals.

15. Flash Sales and Pop-Up Events:
    – Announcing last-minute flash sales.
    – Promotions for walk-ins and pop-up events.
    – Limited-time deals for immediate bookings.

MOTIVATIONAL CONTENT:

1. Inspirational Quotes:
   - Share daily or weekly beauty/hair-related quotes.
   - Quotes about self-love, confidence and inner beauty.
   - Inspirational sayings from beauty icons and influencers.

2. Client Success Stories:
   - Highlight client transformations and their personal journeys.
   - Share testimonials from clients about salon services improving their confidence.
   - Before and after photos with motivational captions.

3. Stylist/Therapist Spotlights:
   - Share stories of your stylists and their career journeys.
   - Highlight their passion for beauty/hair and client care.
   - Motivational messages from stylists to clients.

4. Beauty Challenges:
   - Create and promote beauty challenges (e.g. thirty-day hair care challenge).
   - Encourage followers to participate and share their progress.
   - Offer tips and encouragement throughout the challenge.

5. Self-Care Tips:
  – Share tips on how clients can take care of themselves.
  – Encouragement to take time for personal pampering and relaxation.
  – Tips on balancing beauty routines with overall well-being.

6. Behind-the-Scenes Inspiration:
  – Show behind-the-scenes moments at the salon.
  – Share the dedication and effort your team puts into their work.
  – Motivational messages about the passion behind the beauty industry.

7. Transformation Tuesday:
  – Regular posts featuring dramatic makeovers.
  – Inspirational captions about the power of change and self-improvement.
  – Encourage clients to share their own transformation stories.

8. Beauty Myths Busted:
  – Debunk common beauty myths and misconceptions.
  – Empower clients with accurate information and positive affirmations.
  – Encourage a healthy and realistic approach to beauty.

9. Motivational Videos:

- Short video clips with motivational messages from stylists and clients.
- Time-lapse videos of transformations with uplifting music.
- Client interviews about their beauty journeys.

10. Self-Improvement Tips:

- Advice on setting and achieving personal beauty goals.
- Encouragement to try new styles and step out of comfort zones.
- Tips for building a positive self-image and confidence.

11. Daily Affirmations:

- Share daily affirmations focused on beauty and self-love.
- Encourage followers to repeat and share these affirmations.
- Create beautiful graphics with affirmations for easy sharing.

12. Celebrating Diversity:

- Highlight the beauty of diverse hair types, skin tones, and styles.
- Share stories and images that celebrate individuality.
- Encourage inclusivity and acceptance in the beauty community.

13. Personal Growth Stories:

  - Share stories of personal growth and overcoming challenges.
  - Highlight how beauty routines and self-care can contribute to personal development.
  - Inspirational messages about resilience and perseverance.

14. Community Engagement:

  - Celebrate milestones and achievements within your community.
  - Share uplifting news and events from your local area.
  - Encourage a sense of community and support among your followers.

15. Mindfulness and Beauty:

  - Share tips on incorporating mindfulness into beauty routines.
  - Encouragement to practise gratitude and mindfulness in daily life.
  - Inspirational messages about finding peace and joy in beauty rituals.

TRUST CONTENT:

1. Client Testimonials:
   - Share video or written testimonials from satisfied clients.
   - Highlight specific services and positive experiences.
   - Use authentic, unedited quotes and feedback.

2. Before and After Photos:
   - Showcase real client transformations.
   - Ensure the photos are high-quality and highlight the differences clearly.
   - Include details about the services provided.

3. Team Credentials and Certifications:
   - Introduce your team and highlight their qualifications.
   - Share their certifications, training and professional achievements.
   - Feature their ongoing education and participation in industry events.

4. Behind-the-Scenes Content:
   - Show the day-to-day of the salon.
   - Highlight cleanliness, hygiene practices and attention to detail.
   - Share the preparation and care that goes into each service.

5. Client Stories:

- Share detailed stories of clients' experiences.
- Focus on how your services have positively impacted their lives.
- Include quotes and direct feedback from the clients.

6. Quality Product Features:

- Highlight the professional-grade products used in the salon.
- Share information about the brands and their benefits.
- Explain why these products were chosen and how they enhance the services.

7. Awards and Recognition:

- Share any awards, recognitions or accolades the salon has received.
- Highlight any media features or mentions in reputable sources.
- Display certificates and awards prominently in posts.

8. Service Guarantees:

- Explain any satisfaction guarantees or policies the salon offers.
- Highlight a commitment to client satisfaction and quality.
- Share stories of how issues were resolved promptly and professionally.

9. Client Safety Measures:
   - Detail the safety and hygiene protocols in place.
   - Share updates about adherence to local health regulations.
   - Show behind-the-scenes content of sanitation practices.

10. Expert Tips and Advice:
    - Share professional tips and advice related to hair, skincare and beauty.
    - Provide insights that demonstrate the expertise and knowledge of your team.
    - Engage with followers by answering their questions and offering personalised advice.

11. Community Involvement:
    - Highlight the salon's involvement in local events and charities.
    - Share stories of giving back to the community.
    - Show how the salon supports local causes and organisations.

12. Client Care Stories:
    - Share instances when the salon went above and beyond for clients.
    - Highlight personal touches and exceptional customer service.
    - Encourage clients to share their positive experiences.

13. Transparent Pricing:
  - Clearly outline the pricing for services.
  - Explain what clients can expect for each price point.
  - Share any value-added services included in the pricing.

14. Detailed Service Descriptions:
  - Provide comprehensive descriptions of each service offered.
  - Include information about the process, duration and expected results.
  - Share any preparation or aftercare tips for clients.

15. Real-time Client Feedback:
  - Encourage clients to share their experiences in real time.
  - Respond to client comments and reviews promptly and professionally.
  - Share positive feedback and how you've addressed any concerns.

That is a crazy amount of content right there for you! You're welcome. In fact, let me give you a six-month content plan.

Week	Monday	Wednesday	Friday
1	Hair Care Tips	Client Testimonial	Inspirational Quote
2	Service Highlight	Behind-the-Scenes	Client Success Story
3	Skincare Advice	Team Credential Spotlight	Beauty Challenge Launch
4	Product Recommendation	Client Story	Motivational Video
-	-	-	-
5	Hair Care Tips	Before and After Photos	Inspirational Quote
6	Promotional Offer	Behind-the-Scenes	Transformation Tuesday
7	Makeup Tutorial	Client Testimonial	Self-Care Tip
8	Product Promotion	Team Credential Spotlight	Daily Affirmation
-	-	-	-
9	Skincare Advice	Before and After Photos	Celebrating Diversity
10	Service Highlight	Client Story	Motivational Video
11	Product Recommendation	Behind-the-Scenes	Self-Improvement Tip
12	Client Testimonial	Team Credential Spotlight	Transformation Tuesday
-	-	-	-
13	Hair Care Tips	Before and After Photos	Motivational Quote

14	Promotional Offer	Client Testimonial	Beauty Myths Busted
15	Makeup Tutorial	Behind-the-Scenes	Client Success Story
16	Product Promotion	Team Credential Spotlight	Inspirational Quote
-	-	-	-
17	Skincare Advice	Client Story	Celebrating Diversity
18	Service Highlight	Before and After Photos	Motivational Video
19	Product Recommendation	Behind-the-Scenes	Transformation Tuesday
20	Client Testimonial	Team Credential Spotlight	Self-Care Tip
-	-	-	-
21	Hair Care Tips	Client Story	Inspirational Quote
22	Promotional Offer	Before and After Photos	Beauty Challenge Launch
23	Makeup Tutorial	Behind-the-Scenes	Client Success Story
24	Product Promotion	Team Credential Spotlight	Daily Affirmation
-	-	-	-
25	Skincare Advice	Client Testimonial	Celebrating Diversity
26	Service Highlight	Before and After Photos	Motivational Video

This calendar covers educational, sales, motivational and trust-building content to keep the audience informed, inspired and connected to the salon. The four pillars of content are spread over the six months to ensure a balanced and engaging presence.

You can download this content plan in an easy-to-use form from **www.kgbusinessmentor.com/book**.

Now back to emails….

As long as you cover these four pillars within your emails too, you will produce a good email.

Keep it informative and make it really easy for people to read. I always say, gone are the days of newsletters. A newsletter, like social media, is a one-to-many form of writing, which is why they don't work as well nowadays. I also think the idea of creating a newsletter puts people off sending marketing emails as they seem like so much work, what with making all those pretty emails in Canva. It doesn't have to be like that.

Email like you are emailing a friend. You might add a pretty picture for attention, but otherwise, just write. On social media, everyone knows you are posting to all your followers – but email is one to one which is why it's important to write like you are writing to a friend. Add their name, keep it friendly, have a chat and tell them about your weekend as well as promoting your services. Clients love the personal touch and it makes them feel more part of the brand. Make sure you add a direct link to book the service you want them to book. This makes it simple for the client.

I have developed a love for email marketing and for marketing in general because when I started my salon I had no choice other than to try everything I possibly could.

I opened the doors with not one client. I had never done a client in my life. No one knew who I was. We could say that wasn't the smartest move and I don't recommend opening a salon this way. But I managed to get it to work and I turned out a huge success after the blood, sweat and tears. Most of this was because through willpower and determination, but also because I kept up with my marketing. I tried and tested everything you can think of, but emails were and are gold for me. Every business I start, email marketing is one of the first things I set up and I don't go a week without emailing my clients and customers.

If you're not currently emailing, start doing so every other week and see how you get on. I bet you'll notice a huge difference if you stay consistent.

A potential client needs to consume over seven hours of your content before deciding they trust you and book in. That is pretty nuts, isn't it? That is a lot of content to get out there!

I remember when a client had to see something between four and seven times before they would buy, thinking that was a lot. Then it went up to between seven and fourteen times. Now they need seven hours. This is due to there being so many businesses out there that we all have so much choice. We consume a huge amount of marketing every day. And you need to be the business that stands out and is remembered, not just on social media but across your marketing strategy. And believe it or not, there is so much more to it than socials and emails.

Let me give you a list of ways to market your beauty business. Of course, there are more, but this is my go-to list:

Social media

Email marketing

WhatsApp

Pinterest

A website

SEO

Leaflet drops

Google my business

Online directories

Referral programme

Loyal programme

Collaborations with local businesses

Events and workshops

Print marketing

SMS marketing

Video marketing

Brand merchandise

Influencer

Mobile app

Networking events

Podcasts

PR

Charity and community

Direct mail

Event days/evenings

I bet you said about some of those examples: *I didn't realise that was marketing.* The best way to think about marketing is making yourself visible as many times as you can. How often can you put yourself in front of people? You want to do this as much as possible. Do not be scared about bugging people or putting yourself out there too much.

I don't want you to get overwhelmed, thinking you have so much work to do. But I do want you to act. I suggest you pick seven marketing choices and focus on doing them well. It is better to do a few things brilliantly than do everything not so well. You can always add things when you get used to implementing what you have chosen. Even better, you can add more when you have stepped *out* of your business to work *on* your business.

Let me talk to you about Jade, who owns Ooh La La Lashes and Brows in West Sussex. She started her salon with self-employed staff and worked on clients three days a week around her children, taking in around £4,000 a month. Jade had always been good at social media, which she was using for her marketing. She took my masterclass about stepping out of your business to work on your business. It taught her the importance of working on the business and getting off the salon floor. Jade then came into my Six-Step Proven Method Programme (and saw her salon takings increase hugely) and afterwards into the mastermind! Within a year of the mastermind, Jade more than doubled her income from £7,000 months to £15,000 months.

You're wondering how? Jade made so many changes to Ooh La La Lashes and Brows which helped this income boost. She changed her team from self-employed to employed, added extra services and stepped off the salon floor. The last of these changes was the most important. It gave her the time to be the businesswoman she is. She could grow the business and really look at her marketing strategy, creating a lot more depth than just social media.

Jade looked at the same marketing list I gave you earlier and took on many layers to add to her business. She concentrated on her website, implemented lead magnets, started email and WhatsApp marketing, created salon events and collaborated locally, to name a few. Above all, she had the time to be consistent in her marketing. I am sure you have heard it said many times that consistency is key, but it is true. This world is now such a busy place with so many people promoting their businesses daily that you must get lost amongst everyone else – which will happen if you're not consistent. If you are consistent, you will be at the forefront of people's minds all the time when they think of your industry. This is how you achieve growth.

WEBSITES

It is important to have a website when you have a business. I talk to so many business owners who still don't have a website. Perhaps they are saving up to get one and are using their Instagram page as their site in the meantime. This is a no-no.

Yes, lots of people search Instagram for their new nail tech or the most Instagrammable salon near them, but you must also think about your target audience. Are your target audience all on Instagram? Is this where you make all your salon bookings? I doubt it, but even if it is, imagine what could happen if you gave people more ways to search for you or book appointments.

People still search and always will search on Google (or other search engines) when they need to find something new. Make sure your business comes up on that first page. If it doesn't, you're missing out on business.

If you do have a website, a massive well done for being ahead of the game. But… when did you last update it? If a client landed on your website right now, would they find your up-to-date opening hours, services and pricing? Would they find clear details on the services you offer? Is it easy for them to book using the site? Having a website is all very well, but if it hasn't been updated since you set it up in 2020, that's no good. You need to keep it current.

I learnt how important websites are when I was young. Before I started my salon, I was in the modelling world. I started modelling at thirteen years old and stopped at nineteen when the salon took off. During that time, I had my own model agency – my first ever business. I had models all around the world on my books. As a model and as an agent I had to have a website to get bookings. This was before the days of Facebook and Instagram.

Back then, I learnt about Search Engine Optimisation (SEO). That might sound technical, but it simply means making sure your business shows up when people search online for services like yours. Imagine you run a beauty salon that offers lash extensions, microblading and skincare treatments. When someone types 'lash extensions near me' into Google, you want your business to appear at the top of the results. SEO helps make that happen.

By optimising your website for search engines, you increase your chances of being found by people who are looking for exactly what you offer. Implementing SEO doesn't have to be overwhelming. This is how you can start:

1. Understand Your Audience: Think about what your potential clients are searching for. Are they looking for best microblading in Bedfordshire or organic skincare products? Knowing these search terms (called keywords) is the first step.

2. Use Relevant Keywords: Once you know what your clients are searching for, use those keywords on your website. This could be in your blog posts, service descriptions, or even in the titles of your web pages. For example, if lash extensions Surrey is a popular search term, make sure it appears on your lash extensions service page.

3. Create Quality Content: Google loves fresh, valuable content. Consider starting a blog where you share beauty tips and trends or explain your services. For example, write posts titled "The Benefits of Organic Skincare Products" or "How to Choose the Right Lash Extensions". This signals to search engines that your site is active and relevant, and it also attracts readers when the search engine places it in their results.

4. Optimise Your Website: Make sure your website is user-friendly. It should load quickly and be easy to navigate. It should also look good on mobile devices as everyone searches on their phone nowadays. Search engines prioritise websites that offer a good user experience.

5. Get Listed Locally: Claim your business on Google My Business. This helps your salon appear in local searches, especially when people are looking for services 'near me'. Encourage happy clients to leave reviews: positive feedback boosts your credibility and can improve your ranking.

6. Build Links: When other reputable websites link to your content, search engines see you as an authority in your field. Reach out to local bloggers or beauty influencers to ask if they'll review your services or feature your business on their site.

7. Monitor Your Progress: Use tools like Google Analytics to see how people find your website and which pages are most popular. This data helps you understand what's working and where you can improve.

SEO is an ongoing process, not a one-time task. There are people out there you can pay to work on your SEO for you, but making it work is a long-term investment. If you want to do this yourself rather than outsource it, make sure you block out the time in your diary to do the points above and keep on top of them. It is easier to do if you step away from the salon floor and clients.

As you continue to optimise your site and create valuable content, you'll see your online visibility improve, which brings new clients to you daily. Who wouldn't want that? Remember, your goal is to make it as easy as possible for potential clients to find you when they search for beauty services. With effort and consistency, SEO can become a powerful tool to grow your beauty, hair or aesthetic business.

A little earlier, I mentioned blogging. At its core, blogging involves regularly updating your website with new content in the form of articles or posts. These posts can cover a wide range of topics, from beauty tips and trends to how-to guides, product reviews, and news about your services. Think of your blog as an online journal or magazine, a platform where you can share your expertise, engage with your audience, and keep your website fresh and relevant.

One of the biggest benefits of blogging is its impact on SEO. Each time you publish a new blog post, you give search engines like Google more content to index. This can help your site appear in search results for a wider range of keywords, making it easier for potential clients to find you. For example, if you write a post about "How to Maintain Lash Extensions", your site might show up when someone searches for that topic. The more content you create, the more opportunities you have to attract visitors to your website.

I have found blogging a helpful thing to do in my business not only to improve my SEO but to help my clients learn about us. Blogging enhances your online presence and also connects with your clients on a deeper level and builds their trust in you. It also helps you with your personal brand by establishing you as an authority in the beauty industry. By sharing your knowledge and expertise through your posts, you position yourself as a trusted source of information. Clients are likely to trust and choose your business over one that hasn't done any of this.

Another powerful aspect of blogging is the platform it gives you to connect with your clients beyond your salon or clinic. Through your blog, you can address common questions, share stories or offer insights into the latest beauty trends. This keeps your clients engaged with your brand and encourages them to visit your website more often. The more they interact with your content, the stronger their connection to your business becomes.

While blogging should mainly be focused on providing value, it also is a great way to promote your services. For instance, a post on "The Benefits of Organic Skincare" can naturally lead into a mention of the organic skincare products or treatments you offer. This approach educates your readers while show-casing your services, making it more likely that they'll consider booking an appointment.

As well as driving traffic to your website, blogging supports your social media. Every blog post you publish creates new content you can share across your social media platforms. This keeps your social media feeds active and engaging and also directs your followers back to your website, where they can learn more about your services. The more often you update your blog, the more content you have to share, creating more engagement on your socials and website.

Blogging also builds relationships. It allows for two-way communication between you and your audience. Readers can leave comments, ask questions and share your posts with others, creating a sense of community around your brand. Engaging with your readers in the comments section or through social media reinforces these relationships and shows that you value their input.

Starting a blog for your beauty business doesn't have to be complicated. You are already creating emails for your business, so to make it super simple you can create the e-mail and tweak that into your blog. This is then using one piece of content for two things… even three things when you share that to your social media. This is called repurposing content. Rather than spending hours on blogging, hours on emails and then hours on social media posts, use the same content across everything but tweak it for that platform.

Begin by identifying your audience and thinking about what they are interested in. What questions do they have? What beauty tips are they searching for? The key to creating content is to write about topics that align with your services and resonate with your audience.

Consistency in blogging is crucial. Regular updates to your blog keep your audience engaged and improve your SEO. You can build momentum by sticking to a schedule, whether you choose to post weekly, bi-weekly or monthly.

It is just as important to promote your blog as it is to write it. Share your posts on social media, include them in your emails, and even mention them to your clients in your salon or clinic. The more you promote your content, the more people will see it, and the greater the impact on your business will be.

Let me introduce you to Emma-Jayne from Mirror Mirror in Cleethorpes. I have worked with Emma-Jayne for years. She has come from being a Saturday girl to having her own incredible salon and has grown as a business in so many ways. I taught her lash extensions many years ago, and she has had power hours with me, been part of my membership, and in my mastermind. She has also been a trainer for my lash brand KG Professional.

Emma-Jayne specialises in bridal and wanted to grow this part of the business. One thing she has done really well is blogging. When she started blogging, at first she wrote about her personal stories of the sadness of baby loss. Writing on this subject helped her get her feelings down on paper and also connected her with clients who had gone through or were going through the same. This helped Emma-Jayne make a success of fundraising events she held for her clients and the public, and this in turn built her brand. She then switched her blogging around to her bridal clients, sharing their love stories. What a brilliant idea. Everyone loves a story, so this worked perfectly for her. Through creating these blogs Emma-Jayne has been published in the local papers and the number of visitors to her website grew by 1625%, which is an incredible uptick.

OLD SCHOOL MARKETING

Let me go over some old school marketing, as I would call it. Leafleting, I mean. When I opened my salon, I badly needed to get some clients through the door. I couldn't afford to get a company to leaflet the local houses for me, so I went out on Sundays, Mondays and in the evenings to do it myself. I can't say I enjoyed it, especially the dogs that nearly nipped my fingers when I put the leaflet through or the ones that barked out of nowhere and scared the hell out of me! But it definitely helped me get appointments so I won't complain.

As the years went on, if I needed a fresh influx of clients I did this again. I even perfected my leaflets to convert those who were interested. Later, I could even afford to pay a company to leaflet for me. Bliss!

Leafleting is still powerful, perhaps even more so than years ago when I first started doing it. It is personal and offers no competition. When was the last time you picked up your post and held a salon's or clinic's leaflet? On the other hand, you can scroll on social media tonight and come across ten businesses all fighting for the same customers.

With a leaflet, it is just you in their hands, in their home. Years ago, a newspaper came through the door and tons of leaflets fell out. Now, you receive a couple of bills or that dreaded brown envelope but not many advertising leaflets. This makes it the perfect time to give it a go. However, you need to do this in volume. It's a numbers game. Going out and leafleting one street won't make a huge difference. But leafleting your whole town will. The more houses you hit, the more houses will convert.

As you can see, there are many ways to get your business out there and to get new appointments in your diary. I don't want you to get overwhelmed by the possibilities and end up doing none of it, but I would love you to pick a few of these marketing tactics to work on, implement consistently and see your business grow.

You can also pick up more ways of marketing at those times you know you will need them, such as those natural low times we hit within the industry. November is always a dreaded month. The summer rush is over and people cancel because they are dragging out their treatments until their Christmas appointments or they are feeling the financial pressure of Christmas.

I used to hate this time of year. It's still not my favourite but I really used to hate it. During October and November there used to be days when I was close to bankruptcy… when I had little motivation left to keep this business afloat. The salon was so quiet in the beginning that my dad used to pop in after work to keep me company for a bit. I used to love it because it kept me sane rather than seeing no one from ten in the morning until seven in the evening.

I will never forget the day the clocks went back. I hadn't seen a single client all day. Dad stopped by and we had our catch-up, and when I saw he was about to wrap up to go home, I followed suit.

He said, "Where are you going?"

"Home," I replied. I had forgotten to put the salon clock back. It was only six o'clock and I still had an hour left. An hour might not be long, but to me it felt like a whole day. I wanted to cry. I was sinking further into debt by the minute and just wanted to go home and never see that place again.

You could ask why I didn't leave early if I had no clients. Not a chance. Even today, you will never see my salon closed during the advertised opening hours. Firstly, that would be bad customer service if someone dropped by or called the salon. But back then, I also hoped and prayed that just one client might give us some last-minute income for that day.

If I had known all the marketing tactics that I know today, I would have been in a different position. Don't get me wrong, of course there are still quiet times. That's only natural. However, now that I know how to market my business by being visible in all these ways, even these quiet times are much better than they used to be.

Katie celebrating the one-year anniversary of the salon. When paper diaries and tills were used.

CELEBRATING: Katie Godfrey outside the KG Salon.

Success for super salon

A YOUNG entrepreneur, who left school early due to constant bullying, has just celebrated the first anniversary of her beauty salon business.

Katie Godfrey, who dropped out of Icknield High School aged 13, owns KG Salon in Barton. And since she opened 12 months ago she has seen business boom, with a growing client base. She has also expanded the services on offer at the Bedford Road beauty spot, changing a former photographic studio into a spacious beauty treatment room.

The 20-year-old said: "We used to just do tanning and nails but we've now expanded into full beauty treat-

the cosmetic side like teeth whitening and permanent make up."

Last week, Katie and her staff celebrated KG Salon's first birthday with a grand party for customers.

Visitors to the bash enjoyed free use of sunbeds and spray tans for just £5 as well as food and champagne. All treatments had a 20 per cent discount for the day, and each guest went home with a goodie bag packed with different treats.

Katie, of Kingsdown Avenue in Luton, said: "Hundreds of people came down, we had an amazing turnout."

For more details of the treatment available at the salon, visit the we

Katie hit the headlines achieving one year in business.

4

TIME MANAGEMENT: THE
REALITY OF WORK-LIFE BALANCE

The question I probably get asked the most is how to do it all without burning out. You don't want to work so much that you forget you have a life outside of your business. After all, what's the point of running a business if you can't enjoy your life at the same time?

I'll never forget the time I was working around the clock to set up my franchise. Franchising my salon was my ultimate goal, and I couldn't believe it was finally happening. For those who are not familiar, a franchise is a proven business model that you buy into and run as your own company. Take McDonald's, for example: anywhere in the world, you know exactly what taste, look and experience to expect. McDonald's is the brand, but individual locations are run by franchisees, all following the same business model.

The opening day of my first franchisee's salon (Wokingham, UK) came, and I paid the franchisee a visit and met the team.

It was a surreal moment when I saw our sign above the door. Years of planning, preparation and overcoming setbacks had led to this.

Yet that night, I drove home feeling the emptiest I had ever felt. Everything I had dreamed of had just happened. Everything I had worked so hard for had come to life. But I was sitting alone, wondering if this was it. I had been so focused on achieving growth that I didn't know how to enjoy the success. And that success felt incredibly lonely.

I'm not convinced that a perfect, achievable work-life balance exists. To people who see me juggling so many responsibilities, it seems like I'm managing everything with ease. But I don't always get it right. However, there are strategies I can share that will definitely help.

Before I had children, I was always working. I owned a beauty salon and a hair salon in different locations, ran a training academy, launched a product range, and was setting up the franchise. There were no set start or finish times. I never clock-watched. That was my life. I was young, focused, and had few distractions.

Have you ever referred to your salon or clinic as your 'baby'? I used to say it all the time, but when I had Lola-Rose, I suddenly had a real baby to take care of. I learned a big lesson and perhaps you need to learn it too: Your business is not your baby. It is a business, and you need to treat it like one. Otherwise, your business starts to control you.

When I fell pregnant, I was still seeing clients every day at my beauty salon. I put a great system in place to transition my clients so I could step away and take some maternity leave (if you can even call it that as a business owner). I was off the tools and suddenly had what felt like all the time in the world to work on the business and the brand. But my time management skills were zero. Even though I wasn't tied down with clients anymore and had flexibility in where I could work, the business still had me completely trapped. I micromanaged everything and everyone from afar. I had to learn to manage my time better, delegate effectively, and adopt a CEO mindset. And that changed everything for me.

THE REALITY OF WORK-LIFE BALANCE

We've all been sold the idea of achieving a perfect work-life balance, but the reality is far more complicated. There is no magic formula to keep everything perfectly balanced all the time. We're really working towards a rhythm that works for each of us – a way of managing our time that helps in business and in life.

The idea that you can always maintain a perfect balance between work and life is a myth. Balance is not a static state; it shifts and changes depending on what's happening in your life and business. Some days, work will demand more of your time and energy, and on other days, you need to prioritise rest, family or personal time. The key is to recognise when these shifts need to happen and to allow yourself the flexibility to change accordingly.

Sometimes your business needs to take priority. Whether you're in the middle of launching a new product line, opening a new location, or just navigating the day-to-day challenges of running a business, there will be periods when work takes over. And that's okay. It is part of the journey. During these times, give yourself permission to focus on your business without feeling guilty about not being as present in other areas of your life.

But there will also be times when you need to step back and let life take centre stage. Maybe you need to take that long-overdue holiday, spend quality time with your family, or simply give yourself a break after a particularly intense period at work. These moments are just as important as the hustle, and they're essential for maintaining your energy, creativity and passion for your business.

At those times when your business requires your full focus, it feels like everything else has to take a backseat. Maybe you're launching a new service, opening a new salon, or dealing with a crisis that demands your full attention. It is easy to feel overwhelmed and guilty for not being able to do it all. It is perfectly normal for business to take over at times – the important thing is how you manage it.

During those periods of intense work, you should set clear short-term goals. Break down what needs to be done into manageable tasks and prioritise them based on urgency and impact. This helps prevent that overwhelming feeling of having too much on your plate and ensures you do what will move the needle the most.

Delegation is also crucial. You can't do everything yourself and trying to will only lead to burnout. Trust your team to handle things that don't require your direct involvement. Communicate clearly about your expectations and deadlines. This not only frees up your time but also empowers your team to take ownership of their roles. If you don't have a team, outsource to people who do these roles freelance.

When work takes over, it is equally important to communicate with your loved ones. Let them know what's happening and why you need to focus on the business right now. This transparency helps manage their expectations and reduces the guilt you might feel about not being very present. Remember, this is temporary. Once the intense period is over, you can shift your focus back to your personal life. I find it really helpful to give them the heads up, so they understand. Also, our moods can change when we feel under pressure or miss those closest to us. It is better not to mix together work stress and home life, trying to juggle and multitask, as it just doesn't work. I find it effective to allow myself to be at work with no distractions, and then to be present at home with no work distractions. Trying to do both just doesn't work and causes stress.

Instead of seeking the perfect balance, I encourage you to find your rhythm, a way of managing your time that flows with the demands of your business and life. This rhythm will look different for everyone, and it evolves as your circumstances change.

Ask yourself what your own rhythm means to you. It might mean being home for dinner with the family every night or doing the school runs. It could be taking a day off each week to recharge. Whatever it is, make sure it aligns with your values and priorities.

In the end, work-life balance is less about achieving a perfect split between work and life and more about being intentional with your time. It is about knowing when to push forward and when to pull back and being okay with the natural highs and lows of life and business. What works for you today might not work tomorrow. The goal is to create a lifestyle that allows you to be successful in your business while enjoying the other aspects of your life that matter most.

IDENTIFY YOUR TIME WASTERS

Let's face it, time is the one resource we can't get more of. As a beauty business owner, every minute counts, whether you're working with clients, managing your team, or planning for the future. And yet, no matter how focused or driven you are, there are always time wasters lurking in your day, quietly draining your productivity. In this part of the chapter, we'll dig into these sneaky distractions, identify where you lose time, and figure out how to eliminate these time-wasting habits so you can make the most of every hour.

The first step to manage your time is to recognise where you *spend* your time. It is easy to get caught up in small tasks or distractions that feel urgent but don't contribute to your business's success. These time wasters can add up, leaving you feeling like you've worked all day but accomplished very little. You should be doing the money-making tasks: the things that make you money by you doing them or by working towards them. If they are not, don't do them.

TIME-WASTING HABITS

So, how can you spot time-wasters in your daily routine?

1. The Social Media Black Hole

We all know social media is important for marketing your beauty, hair or aesthetics business, but let's be honest, how often do you hop on Instagram to post a client's before-and-after photos, only to find yourself still scrolling sixty minutes later? Social media is designed to keep us engaged, but that engagement can quickly turn into wasted time if you're not careful.

Instead of posting in real-time, use social media scheduling tools to plan your content in advance. At the time of writing

I recommend Business Suite or Instagram itself. Other third-party tools can sometimes affect your reach.

Allocate times in your day for social media and set a timer to keep yourself on track. Once the timer goes off, log out and move on to your next task. You can even turn off notifications on your phone so you do not find yourself jumping online outside your timed sessions. I also suggest that, when you do find yourself scrolling, you at least make it beneficial and comment at least three words on all the posts you see, so it builds your engagement and page rather than unnecessary scrolling which won't benefit you at all and will create an emotional mess of comparison with others.

2. Multitasking Mayhem

Multitasking sounds like a great idea: you're getting more done at once, right? Unfortunately, there is no such thing as multitasking. Your brain cannot do two things at the same time and do either of them well. When we try, it often leads to mistakes, half-finished tasks and wasted time switching between activities. It can actually slow you down and make you less efficient.

Focus on one task at a time. Prioritise your tasks and tackle them one at a time. You will find that you complete each task more quickly and with better results when you don't try to divide your attention.

Batch similar tasks together, like responding to emails or returning voicemails from missed phone calls in the morning, and handle them in one go. This reduces the mental energy you spend switching between different types of work and allows you to complete tasks more efficiently.

Also, get into the habit of time blocking. Set time limits to work on specific tasks. When we give ourselves a time limit, we naturally work within that time frame and get things done faster. If we have no deadline for a task, it takes longer to do. Work in time blocks of thirty, sixty or ninety minutes.

I have always done this with my team in the salon too to help them speed up on treatments. This doesn't mean rushing treatments or cutting corners, but long treatment times are a major reason for salons and clinics being unprofitable. Let's take lash extensions, for example. Creating a set of classic lashes takes me sixty minutes. When someone is training they are slower, of course. However, when a staff member then starts to do models to gain experience and you give them no end time, that staff member will take hours to do that set of lashes. Because they have the time. This then means it is extremely hard to get that staff member's time down. They will panic and feel there is no way they can do it faster. If you give the staff member ninety minutes and tell them to do what they can within that time frame, they will naturally speed up as they know they are working to the clock.

3. The Perfectionism Trap

While it's important to deliver high-quality work, it's also crucial to see when good is good enough.

Perfectionism can be a serious time waster. And we in our industry are known to be perfectionists. Whether it's obsessing over the details of a client's haircut, spending hours tweaking your website, or rewriting an email draft five times, the pursuit of perfection can eat up valuable time that could be better spent elsewhere.

To help, give yourself a reasonable amount of time to complete a task and stick to it. Once the time is up, move on, even if the task isn't entirely perfect.

Have a 'progress over perfection' mindset. Focus on making progress rather than achieving perfection. Done is better than perfect, especially when it comes to managing a busy beauty business.

Try to delegate when possible. If you find yourself getting bogged down in perfectionism, consider delegating tasks to others who can complete them to a high standard without the same level of over-analysis.

4. Unplanned Interruptions

Business owners commonly face constant interruptions throughout the day. I like to call it firefighting. Perhaps a team member calls in sick when she has a column full of clients. Maybe a client drops by without an appointment or an urgent email pulls you away from your work. While some interruptions are unavoidable, many can be managed more effectively to protect your time.

You could create 'office hours' for your team. Set specific times during the day when your team knows you're available for questions or discussions. Outside of these hours, encourage them to handle issues on their own or wait until they know you are available. For example, my team know I'm not available to be contacted after 3.30pm as I'm on school runs and sorting out bedtime routines, which I am not going to try and multitask with or it will end in one big stress ball of either shouting at the kids or being snappy with the team. They know that they should only contact me outside of salon hours if it's about a staff absence the next day.

Set boundaries with clients about when and how they can contact you outside of their appointments. Encourage them to schedule appointments in advance rather than dropping by unexpectedly, and to make online bookings rather than messaging through Facebook Messenger. It is difficult when you are contactable through all streams of media, email and phone, but it doesn't mean you have to be available. Try to streamline how clients can make bookings so it is easy for you to manage.

You can also utilise tools like email filters, do-not-disturb settings on your phone and scheduling apps to minimise unplanned interruptions and keep you focused on your priorities.

THE IMPACT OF PERFECTIONISM ON TIME MANAGEMENT

Perfectionism deserves its own spotlight because it's one of the most insidious time wasters out there. On the surface, striving for perfection might seem like a good thing; after all, you want your work to be the best it can be. But perfectionism often leads to overthinking, procrastination and a fear of failure that paralyses you from making progress.

While it is admirable to aim for excellence, it's important to recognise when perfectionism is doing more harm than good. You might find yourself spending far too much time on a single task, perhaps perfecting a client's look, reworking a service menu or constantly revising your website. In the beauty industry, where precision and attention to detail are highly valued, it's easy to fall into the perfectionism trap.

Why Perfectionism Hurts Your Time Management:

- It slows you down. Even simple tasks take much longer than necessary because you constantly second-guess yourself and redo work that's already good enough.

- It leads to procrastination. The fear of not getting something perfect can cause you to put off a task altogether, which means you're not making progress on your goals.
- It causes stress and burnout. Constantly striving for perfection is exhausting and can lead to burnout, which crushes your productivity and effectiveness.

Overcoming Perfectionism:
- Embrace imperfection. No one is perfect, and that includes you. Accept that mistakes are part of the learning process and that you don't have to be flawless to deliver high-quality work.
- Set realistic standards. Achievable standards for your work allow you to deliver excellence without getting caught up in perfectionism. Remember, your clients appreciate your expertise and care, not your perfection.
- Focus on the big picture. Ask yourself if spending extra time on a task really contributes to your long-term goals. If not, move on and prioritise tasks that will impact your business more.

Stopping any time-wasting habits is a must for improving your productivity and making the most of your time as a business owner. By recognising where you lose time, whether it's through social media distractions, multitasking, perfectionism or unplanned interruptions, you can take control of your day and focus on what matters. Remember, your time is a valuable resource that you cannot get back. Manage it wisely to achieve your business goals while maintaining a healthy work-life balance.

EFFECTIVE TIME MANAGEMENT STRATEGIES

Your day is often filled with doing treatments, managing the team and marketing tasks, not to mention your personal life. Balancing all these responsibilities can be challenging, and it can feel like you're being pulled from pillar to post. With the right time management strategies, you can structure your day to maximise productivity and make sure you focus on those money-making tasks… growing the business.

Not all tasks are created equal: some drive your business forward, while others fill up your day without adding much value and just give you a tick off the to-do list. Prioritisation helps you put first the most important tasks that will have the biggest impact on your business.

1. THE EISENHOWER MATRIX: URGENT VS. IMPORTANT

One of the most effective tools for prioritising tasks is the Eisenhower Matrix, in which you categorise tasks based on their urgency and importance. The matrix divides tasks into four quadrants:

Quadrant 1: Urgent *and* Important
These tasks require your immediate attention. They are crisis situations, urgent client requests, staff sickness, complaints. Handle these tasks first.

Quadrant 2: Important but *not* Urgent
These tasks are critical for your long-term success but don't require immediate action. This could include planning, email

marketing, planning team meetings and training. They often get neglected so make sure to schedule time for them.

Quadrant 3: Urgent but *not* Important

These tasks are distracting and time-consuming but don't significantly contribute to your goals. Examples might include the team messaging you about everything, email checking and replies, or getting back to messages on socials. Delegate or minimise these tasks whenever possible.

Quadrant 4: Not Urgent *and* not Important

These tasks are often time wasters. Social media scrolling, unnecessary meetings or busywork. Eliminate these tasks to free up more time for what really matters.

Using the Eisenhower Matrix allows you to quickly assess your tasks and decide where to focus your energy. The goal is to spend more time in Quadrant 2, working on tasks that are important but not urgent, thus reducing the number of urgent tasks in the future.

2. THE 80/20 RULE

The 80/20 rule suggests that eighty percent of your results come from twenty percent of your efforts. This means a small portion of your work is responsible for the majority of your success. Focusing on these high-impact tasks can significantly improve your productivity.

- Look at Your high-impact activities. Look at your business and see which tasks bring you the best results. Is it when you focus on marketing, when you boost the team in a team meeting or when you go to a local event or spend time connecting with other local businesses? Whatever it is, make these tasks your top priority.

- Eliminate or delegate the rest. Once you've identified the twenty percent of tasks that drive the majority of your success, focus on those and consider eliminating, automating or delegating the other eighty percent that don't contribute as much to your goals.

By concentrating your efforts on the most impactful tasks, you'll achieve better results *and* free up time to focus on the growth of the business with the money-making tasks.

3. THE 'BIG ROCKS' CONCEPT

This is another great strategy to put in place. Imagine a jar that you need to fill with big rocks, pebbles and sand. If you start with the sand and pebbles, there won't be room for the big rocks. But if you put the big rocks in first, the smaller items will fill the gaps around them. Focus on your most important tasks – your 'big rocks' – before anything else.

- What are your big rocks? Figure out the key tasks that will move your business forward each day or week. These could be scheduling your e-mail marketing and social posts, strategic planning or updating your website.
- Schedule these first. Block out time in your calendar for these big rocks before anything else. Getting them done at the beginning of the day also helps. This makes sure that your most important tasks get the attention they need, without being squeezed out by smaller, less important tasks. Do not keep putting them to the back of the list because they feel harder or bigger.

By dealing with your big rocks first, you'll spend your time on the tasks that matter most, helping you to grow the business in line with your goals.

MY SUPER STRUCTURED ROUTINE THAT WILL WORK FOR YOU

I live by routines and structure: it's the backbone of good time management. It is the only way to succeed when running businesses, children and a home. It provides you with a roadmap for your day, helps you stay on track and makes sure you spend time on the right things. Here are the things I do.

TIME BLOCKING:

This is a powerful game changer. Divide your day into blocks of time, each dedicated to a certain task. Start with your priorities. Block out time for those high-priority tasks that need your full attention –your big rocks. Schedule these tasks during your most productive hours, whether that's first thing in the morning or later in the day.

Group together similar tasks such as admin work, staff meetings or marketing activities. This helps you stay in the same mindset and complete tasks more efficiently. Don't forget to schedule breaks and buffer time between tasks so you can recharge and transition smoothly from one activity to the next. It is really important that when your time is up, you move on to the next even if you're not finished. This will speed you up when working on each task too.

DAILY AND WEEKLY PLANNING:

This gives you a clear focus on your goals for the day/week and makes sure that you use your time effectively. By planning your days and weeks in advance, you avoid last-minute scrambling and cover your important tasks in advance.

At the beginning of each week, take some time to review your weekly goals and priorities. See what your big rocks are for the week and schedule them first. Then, fill in the rest of your schedule with other tasks and appointments.

Each evening or first thing in the morning, review your schedule for the day ahead and make changes if you need to. Check your top three priorities for the day and focus on completing them first.

USING DIGITAL TOOLS FOR SCHEDULING:

There are many digital tools available that can help you create and manage your never-ending to-do list more effectively. Whether you prefer a simple calendar app or a more advanced project management tool, these can help you stay organised and on track.

Popular Scheduling Tools:

- Google Calendar or your iPhone calendar. A straightforward, easy-to-use calendar app that allows you to schedule tasks, set reminders and sync across devices. My life is guided by my phone calendar.

- Asana. A advanced project management tool that offers task tracking, deadlines and collaboration features. You can also add your team to it. I use this in a really basic way and plan all my marketing on there. I can see what's going out and what needs to be done. It definitely helps me stay on track.

- Business Suite/Instagram. Perfect to schedule your Instagram and Facebook posts so you don't need to put content out there every day if you're not feeling up to it. Try to schedule a couple of weeks in advance so things like this are automated.

By using these tools to structure your day and week, you'll find it easier to stay organised and manage your time effectively.

QUEEN OF DELEGATION

As a small business owner, it's easy to fall into the trap of trying to do everything yourself. But you can't and you shouldn't. The skill of delegation allows you to free up your time to focus on what you do best, and lets your team take on more responsibility, which they will really like.

Delegation isn't just about offloading jobs: it's about trusting others to help you achieve your business goals. This isn't easily done when most of us are control freaks when it comes to our businesses. By handing over tasks that don't need your personal attention, you can focus on the high-impact tasks, the money-making jobs that will drive your business forward. If you give tasks to those with skills in those areas, you will get better results and faster success. Delegation also gives your team members the opportunity to grow, take ownership of their roles and develop new skills, which can boost morale and productivity.

But what should you delegate and who to?
Not everything can or should be delegated. You need to see what others can handle, whether that's a team member or an outsourced specialist.

Things you can consider delegating are:

Admin work. Tasks like booking appointments, managing emails or bookkeeping can often be handled by someone on reception or a virtual assistant.

Client treatments. This is the most significant way to step out of the business *and* earn much more money. It means you can grow the business faster.

Marketing. Social media management, content creation and email marketing can be outsourced to a marketing professional or a team member.

Stock control and ordering. Doing stock checks, ordering supplies and managing stock levels can be delegated to a trusted team member.

How do you even start to delegate?

To delegate you need clear communication, trust and the ability to let go. Yes, you need to let go of the inner control freak!

Look at your team if you have one yet, and see who has the most experience and is the person you trust to handle some of these tasks. If you don't have a team yet or if you feel no one is suitable, you definitely need to start recruiting.

When you hand a task over, make sure you train the team member to take over successfully.

At this point, many people say, "I haven't got the time to do this," or, "I might as well do it myself: by the time I explain it, I could have done it myself." Yes, in that moment you are correct, but look at the long game. Once this person knows and understands this role, you no longer have to do it. Short-term training and time for long-term gain.

You also need to offer ongoing support until they are confident. For example, in my salon, we do a weekly stock check every Wednesday. A team member goes around the salon, does the stock check and makes sure the system is right. Once this is done, they tell the manager and she then checks the stock levels and orders what is needed. She can order what they need within her monthly budget.

I used to carve out hours to do this all myself when I could have been doing something else that would have progressed the business. I trained the team and the manager over a few weeks to do each of the steps, then I let go and they took over this role. It was important in the beginning to allow them to make mistakes. I gave them examples of what I would have done differently. Now, it is done smoothly each week and I don't even need to double check.

Don't forget your self-care as part of your time management

Time management isn't only about how you structure your workday or prioritise your tasks. It is also about making sure you have the energy, mental clarity and well-being to sustain that level of productivity. It is easy to fall into the trap of always focusing on your business and neglecting yourself. I see this happen all the time and have done it myself too. But if you don't take care of your physical and mental health, your productivity will eventually suffer and so will your business. You need to look after number one, which is you! Not the business and not even your children. Without you, your business can't run: you can't look after your children, family or teams if you aren't well or looked after.

SELF-CARE ISN'T SELFISH

There is a common misconception that taking time for yourself is a luxury or worse... selfish. But here's the truth: self-care is not only essential, it's non-negotiable if you want to run a successful business. When you're constantly running on empty, your ability to make clear decisions, stay creative, and manage your team and clients will disappear.

I know a lot of you struggle with putting yourselves first, so let's think of self-care as maintenance for your most important business asset: you. Just as you wouldn't neglect the upkeep of your salon or laser machine, you can't afford to neglect your own well-being. If you're burnt out, exhausted, or stressed it's impossible to show up fully for your clients or run your business efficiently.

Let me give you some reasons why self-care is essential to effective time management:

- Increased focus. Regular self-care reduces mental fatigue and enhances your ability to concentrate. This means you spend less time procrastinating or getting distracted and more time actually getting things done.
- Better decision-making. When you're well-rested and less stressed, you're able to think clearly and make better business decisions.
- Sustained energy. Taking breaks and incorporating self-care into your routine helps you recharge. As a result, you're more likely to sustain your energy throughout the day without feeling drained.
- Prevention of burnout. Perhaps most importantly, self-care prevents burnout. When you work constantly without taking time to rest and reset, you set yourself up for long-term exhaustion and reduced productivity.

I get it. You're busy. Finding time for self-care may seem impossible or even another thing to add to the list. But the good news is that self-care doesn't have to mean long holidays or even a whole day off (although those are great too). It means building small, consistent practices into your daily or weekly routine that allow you to refresh and destress.

Here are some ways to add in self-care into your routine without feeling like you're taking time away from your business.

SET BOUNDARIES WITH WORK:

One of the biggest challenges for business owners is knowing when to stop working. Even now, I find this one of the hardest things to do. Sometimes I get it really right, but then fall off and need to start again. It is also really difficult when you love your work so much. I believe that my work is part of my self-care too as it makes me happy, but despite that, I need time to stop. It is easy to get caught up in responding to client messages late at night or thinking about the next day's to-do list, but setting boundaries between work and your personal life is a must for your well-being.

Choose a time each day to stop working and stick to it. This could be when the salon closes, so you clock off as soon as you lock that door. Or it could be a personal decision to end work at seven in the evening so you have time to relax.

Have certain times or areas of your life as work-free zones. For example, no checking emails during dinner, or no business discussions after eight. Mine is no work between school pickups and children's bedtimes. Also, I make sure I completely switch off and rest at weekends.

Let your team and clients know your working hours and when you're available. Setting these expectations will make it easier for you to switch off and take time for yourself.

PRIORITISE PHYSICAL HEALTH:

Physical well-being plays a massive role in how productive and energised you feel throughout the day. When you're healthy and active, it's easier to focus on your business and tackle any fires you need to put out during the day.

You need to do regular exercise. I'm not saying you have to hit the gym every morning, but it's amazing if you do! Even a twenty-minute walk or a quick yoga session can make a huge difference to how you feel physically and mentally. It doesn't have to be time-consuming either. Find something that fits into your routine and stick with it. I love getting up in the morning a little earlier than the kids so I can fit in a home workout. It makes me feel so much better and sets me up for the day.

Fuel your body with healthy, nourishing food and stay hydrated to keep your energy levels up throughout the day. I know it's easy to give in to the temptation to skip lunch to fit more clients in. I remember those days of living on energy drinks and chocolate. But good nutrition is important to keep up your stamina.

Then you have to sleep, which is the ultimate self-care practice. It is during sleep that your body and brain recover. Lack of sleep can severely impact your ability to make decisions, stay focused and manage stress. Aim for seven to nine hours of sleep per night and try to have a consistent bedtime routine. I definitely won't tell you to be one of those entrepreneurs living on three hours sleep a night. It is not sustainable and can have long-term negative health effects.

SCHEDULE DOWNTIME:

We often think of self-care as something we do when we're burnt out, but true self-care is proactive, not reactive. Scheduling regular downtime, even if it's just an hour here or there, helps prevent burnout and keeps you on top form. Taking time to rest and recharge also allows creative solutions and new ideas to come to you more easily than when you're constantly stressed or fatigued.

Take short breaks throughout the day. Step away from your salon or clinic, go outside, or simply take a few deep breaths to clear your mind. Even a break of five or ten minutes can help you reset and refocus.

Make sure you block out time in your calendar for rest days, holidays or afternoons when you don't have any clients or work to do. Time off allows you to fully recharge. We are so good at putting everyone first or booking all the appointments that when we do want a break we are fully booked. Book your own time off first that you want throughout the year, then arrange your treatment diary around it. This is so much easier to do when you come off the tools, too.

MENTAL HEALTH SELF-CARE:

Taking care of your mental health is as important as your physical health, especially as a business owner. The mental and emotional demands of running any business can be overwhelming at times, so it's essential to find ways to protect your mental well-being.

Practising mindfulness or meditation can help reduce stress and anxiety while also improving your focus and clarity. Even five minutes of mindfulness practice a day, perhaps as part of your morning routine, can make a significant difference.

I also love journalling. It makes such a huge impact on the mind. Journalling can help you process emotions, reflect on your successes and clear mental clutter. It is also a great way to track your progress, both personally and professionally. I do this in the morning with my daughter Lola-Rose. It is a great thing to do with your children if you have them. Write down your thoughts, feelings or goals. You could even write about what you have done that day or the things you are grateful for.

Make time to connect with friends, family, and loved ones. I think we underestimate social self-care and being around others. Whether it's a quick chat or a longer catch-up, staying connected to others can help reduce feelings of isolation and keep you grounded.

When you carry out self-care, you're not only doing yourself a favour, you're benefitting your business. Regular self-care keeps you energised and focused so you can get more done in less time. When you feel good, you work better. When you're well-rested and mentally clear, you're able to show up fully for your clients or teams. You will be more present, more patient and more attentive, which leads to stronger relationships and higher client satisfaction.

Running a beauty business is a long-term game. Burnout is one of the biggest threats to your longevity. By taking care of yourself now, you're investing in the long-term success of your business.

TIME MANAGEMENT CHALLENGES

Life and business are unpredictable. Even with the best time management strategies in place, challenges will always happen. No matter how well you plan, there will be disruptions. Managing this without losing momentum can be really hard at times but you can learn how to do it.

While a structured routine is important, it's equally important to stay flexible. Your plan for the day might change, and that's okay. You can get back to the routine tomorrow. This can be really hard when you're still doing clients in the salon, but if you start coming off the tools, doing fewer hours working on clients, it will make this easier.

If something comes up, look at your priorities. Ask yourself: What absolutely must get done today, and what can be postponed? Focus on what's urgent and important. Move less critical tasks to another time. Easier said than done, I know, but panicking when something happens like a staff member calling in sick on a fully booked day only makes things worse. It always helps me to say, "This feeling is temporary." Take a deep breath, assess the situation and adjust your plan accordingly. Staying calm allows you to think clearly and find solutions quickly. As a business owner, it's easy to feel like you need to handle every issue yourself, but that's not true. If you have a team, lean on them during any challenges. If a last-minute issue arises that you need to resolve yourself, delegate some other tasks so you can focus on resolving the issue.

Trust your team. They are there to support you so use them. Empower them to make decisions on their own when necessary. If you trust your team to handle smaller issues, you'll have more time to resolve bigger challenges.

STAYING MOTIVATED AND FOCUSED

Time management is not only about how you structure your time. It is about staying motivated even when challenges come up. Motivation can waver, especially when you're juggling multiple responsibilities, but there are things you can do to keep your energy and motivation high.

Set small, achievable goals. Big goals are important, but they can also feel overwhelming. Break down your larger objectives into smaller, manageable tasks that you can achieve in a short amount of time. This creates a sense of accomplishment and keeps you motivated to tackle the next task.

If your goal is to launch a new service, for example, break it down into smaller tasks like researching products, setting up marketing and training your staff. Complete each step one by one instead of trying to do everything at once.

When you achieve a small goal, take a moment to celebrate. It could be as simple as ticking off a task on your to-do list or taking a short break to reflect on your progress. Celebrating these wins helps build momentum.

Try to stay connected to your 'why'. On tough days, when it feels like the tasks never end, reconnecting with your deeper purpose can help you push through. Why did you start your beauty business? What excites you about helping clients feel confident and beautiful? Keep your 'why' at the forefront of your mind to remind you of the bigger picture and help you stay motivated.

Ways to stay connected to your purpose:

- Vision board. Create a vision board that shows your goals and why you're working so hard. Include pictures, words or symbols that remind you of what you're aiming for and place it somewhere you will see it daily.

- Reflect on client impact. When your motivation dips, remember the impact your services have on your clients. Reflect on positive feedback and the difference you make in their lives. This can help you find your passion, even on difficult days. I have a folder on my phone full of reviews and testimonies for when I feel a little *meh* and need a boost to feel connected again.

At the end of the day, time management is about making intentional choices. You have the power to decide how you spend your time, what you prioritise, and how you balance the demands of work and life. This is *your* business and *your* life. There will always be challenges, but with the right strategies in place you can create a routine that works for you – one that allows you to grow your business while still enjoying the life you've worked so hard to build.

Your time is valuable. Don't let it slip away on distractions or unimportant things. Use the tools and techniques in this chapter to take control of your diary, manage your energy and focus on what really matters. By doing so, you'll not only create a more productive business, you'll carve out the space to enjoy the journey and take care of yourself along the way.

5

MONEY MINDSET: WHAT'S STOPPING YOU FROM GROWING?

When we talk about the success of your beauty business, we often focus on practical things such as marketing, client retention, service quality and so on. But there's a deeper, often overlooked factor that plays a massive role in determining whether your business will be a success or struggle: your money mindset.

A lot of your business success comes from your money mindset. It can hold you back or skyrocket you. Your money mindset usually stems from your childhood and what you were told about money. If your parents or caregivers were good with money, great at saving, and had healthy financial habits, then we are likely to develop similar attitudes as we grow up. On the other hand, if they were bad with money, in debt, and had no savings, the chances are you might follow that lead.

I'm sure you've heard sayings like, "Money doesn't grow on trees," or, "Money is the root of all evil," growing up. These beliefs play a huge part in shaping how we manage money day to day, often planting seeds of fear, scarcity or guilt. If you're a parent, bear in mind the language you use with your children about money, so they can grow up with a healthy relationship with money rather than a negative one.

But what if you're now realising you have a bad relationship with money? Maybe you struggle with saving, feel anxious about spending, or believe that wealth is out of reach for you. Don't worry, you can work on this and changed it with some effort and awareness, which we will go over together in this chapter.

I believe money is an exchange of energy – a tool. I don't subscribe to the idea that money makes people evil or greedy. I see money as a magnifier of who we already are. For example, let's talk about lottery winners. If someone wins the lottery and is naturally a generous, kind person, they are likely to use their newfound wealth to give more to charity and help others. On the other hand, if someone is naturally greedy or self-centred, more money might only heighten those traits.

Mastering your money mindset is a crucial step toward achieving your goals. In this chapter, we'll talk about understanding what a money mindset is, where it comes from, and how it influences every aspect of our lives and businesses. We will also explore how you can identify and overcome your limiting beliefs about money, change your mindset, and use money as a tool for growth, freedom and positive impact.

So, what exactly is a money mindset? Simply put, it's the set of beliefs and attitudes you hold about money. It is how you think and feel about earning, spending, saving and investing. Your money mindset shapes every financial decision you make, from how you price your services to how you invest in growing your business.

TYPES OF MONEY MINDSET

Let's break it down a bit further by looking at the two primary types of money mindset: scarcity mindset and abundance mindset.

SCARCITY MINDSET

A scarcity mindset is rooted in the belief that there's never enough. If you've ever found yourself thinking, "I can't afford that," or, "There's no way I'll ever make that much money," you're experiencing a scarcity mindset. If you ever got told when you were younger that money doesn't grow on trees, you might have the belief that there is a lack of money out there for you to have, which can stop you earning what you really want to earn from this business. This type of thinking can make you overly cautious, afraid to take risks, or reluctant to invest in your business. You might constantly worry about money, feel anxious when bills are due, or even hesitate to charge what your services are truly worth because you fear clients won't pay.

Scarcity thinking can hold you back in many ways. For example, you might underprice your services because you believe that's the only way to attract clients. Or, you might avoid investing in better products, equipment or a mentor because you're too focused on what you might lose rather than what you could gain.

ABUNDANCE MINDSET

On the other hand, an abundance mindset is based on the belief that there's plenty to go around. When you have an abundance mindset, you trust that money will flow in as needed, and you're more likely to see opportunities rather than obstacles. This doesn't mean being reckless or ignoring financial realities, but it does mean having confidence in your ability to attract wealth and grow your business.

With an abundance mindset, you're more likely to invest in your business, whether that's through better marketing, advanced training or upgrading your salon space. You understand that money is a tool rather than something you need to keep hold of it to stop horrible things happening. You know that there is more money out there. When used wisely, money can help you achieve your goals and create more freedom and opportunities.

Your money mindset doesn't only affect your personal finances, it directly impacts how you run your business. If you operate from a place of scarcity, it can show up in subtle ways that may hold your business back. For example, you might:

- set prices too low because you're afraid clients won't pay more, even though your services are worth it.
- avoid investing in growth such as not hiring a staff member or upgrading your equipment because you're worried about spending the money.
- feel stuck or overwhelmed, constantly stressing about cash flow, which makes it hard to focus on the bigger picture and long-term planning.

On the flip side, a positive money mindset can lead to powerful changes in how you look at your business. When you believe in abundance, you're more likely to:

- charge what you're worth, confidently setting prices that reflect the value you provide, knowing that the right clients, your ideal clients, will see the value and pay for it.

- invest in growth, understanding that spending money on your business (e.g. on marketing, staff, equipment or a coach/mentor) is an investment in your future success.
- stay calm and focused, trusting that money will flow in as needed, allowing you to make decisions from a place of confidence rather than fear.

Before you read further, take a moment to reflect on your thoughts and feelings about money. Do you often feel stressed or anxious about your finances? Do you avoid looking at your bank account or bank statements? Or do you feel confident and proactive about managing your money and making money decisions?

It is important to recognise where you currently stand. Understanding your money mindset is the first step toward transforming it. It is okay if you recognise some scarcity thinking in yourself; most people do. The key thing is that you're aware of it and ready to make changes.

Your money mindset is a powerful force that influences every part of your beauty business. By understanding whether you're operating from a place of scarcity or abundance, you can make intentional changes that will support your growth and success.

WHERE DID YOUR MONEY MINDSET COME FROM?

Your money mindset didn't just appear out of nowhere. It has been shaped over time by a variety of influences: your upbringing, your personal experiences, and even the society and people around you. When you understand where your money mindset comes from, you can recognise how it might affect your business decisions today.

CHILDHOOD INFLUENCES:

For many of us, our first lessons about money came from our parents or caregivers. As children, we were like sponges, soaking up everything we heard and saw, including how the adults around us handled money. Whether we realised it or not, those early experiences shaped our beliefs about money – beliefs that often stick with us into adulthood.

Think back to your childhood. What common phrases did you hear about money? Maybe you heard things like, "Money doesn't grow on trees," or, "We can't afford that." These seemingly harmless phrases can sow seeds of scarcity and fear. On the other hand, if you grew up in a household where money was talked about openly and positively, you might have a more confident and abundant view of finances.

As a mum, I catch myself nearly saying some of these scarcity mindset phrases around Lola-Rose and Brodee. I mean, it's so hard sometimes when children are *want, want, want,* and have no awareness of money. But I always try to rephase what I feel like saying. I might say things like, "We can save our money and get something more special later," or, "We are learning to use money more wisely."

I am trying to teach them about money day to day so they develop a good money mindset as they grow up. I opened them both bank accounts when they were born and over the years their savings have grown. I have put away their birthday money, Christmas money and money they have earned by doing little chores or coming to the salon for the day with mummy. It is very cute when they receive money. They now say to me, "Mummy, I will spend half and save half," as that's what I have taught them since babyhood in hope they will be good at managing money when they are older.

Imagine you grew up in a household where your parents always saved money and avoided unnecessary spending. This might have instilled a strong sense of financial caution in you – perhaps so strong that now, as a business owner, you hesitate to invest in things that could help your business grow, like high-quality products, advanced training or marketing.

Alternatively, if you were raised in an environment where money was spent freely with little thought for the future, you might find yourself struggling with cash flow or dealing with the stress of financial instability in your business.

Those early experiences might be influencing your current money mindset. If certain beliefs are holding you back, it's important to acknowledge where they come from and understand that you have the power to change them.

CULTURAL AND SOCIAL INFLUENCES:

Beyond our immediate family, the culture and society we grow up in also play a significant role in shaping our money mindset. Different cultures have different attitudes toward money, wealth and success, and these views can impact how we think about money in our own lives.

In some cultures, discussing money openly is considered taboo, leading to a lack of financial knowledge and confidence in handling money matters. In other cultures, wealth and success are celebrated, which might encourage a more positive and ambitious approach to money.

As a beauty business owner, you might also be influenced by social norms and expectations within the industry itself. The beauty industry can sometimes place a high value on appearances and status, which might lead to pressure to have a certain image or to invest heavily in the look and feel of your salon, even at the expense of financial stability.

Consider the views you've received from society about what it means to be successful in the beauty industry. Have these views encouraged you to spend beyond your means in order to 'keep up' with competitors? Have they instilled a belief in you that making money in this industry is difficult or only achievable for a select few? Or that clients won't pay over a certain price for a service?

PERSONAL EXPERIENCES:

Your money mindset is also shaped by your personal experiences. These could include major life events, such as losing a job, starting your own business, dealing with debt or even achieving a big turnover milestone.

For beauty professionals, personal experiences in the industry can be particularly influential. For example, if you've experienced clients who don't want to pay what you are worth, this might lead to a mindset of constantly undervaluing your services, afraid that clients will walk away if you charge more.

On the other hand, if you've experienced the rewards of investing in yourself, perhaps by investing in a coach who significantly improved your knowledge and income, you might have a more positive and proactive approach to investing in your business.

Take some time to reflect on the key money experiences that have shaped your journey. Did a particular setback make you more cautious? Did a success story give you the confidence to take bigger risks? You can recognise patterns in your money mindset once you understand how these experiences have influenced you.

Let's identify and challenge any limiting beliefs that might be
holding you back. These are the beliefs that keep you stuck
in a scarcity mindset, prevent you from charging what you're
worth or make you hesitant to invest in your business.

Start by asking yourself these key questions:

- What do I believe about money that might not be
  serving me?
- How do these beliefs show up in my business
  decisions?
- Where did these beliefs come from? Are they truly
  valid?

Use your workbook at **www.kgbusinessmentor.com/book** to
guide you on this.

For example, if you believe 'money is hard to come by', you
might hesitate to invest in marketing, fearing that the investment won't pay off. However, by challenging this belief and
replacing it with a more empowering one, such as 'money flows
to me when I provide value', you can shift your mindset and
open up new opportunities for growth.

By recognising how your childhood, cultural and personal
experiences have shaped your beliefs about money, you can
start to identify any limiting beliefs that might be holding you
back as a business owner. Remember, these beliefs are not set
in stone: you can challenge and change them.

COMMON MONEY MINDSET BLOCKS

From setting prices to making investment decisions, your money mindset plays a significant role in how you run your business. However, many of us carry around hidden blocks that sabotage our success. I love going through this with my clients to discover their personal money blocks and to break them down so they can work on them, which then changes the growth of their business. Let's work our way through various money mindset blocks and how to overcome them.

1. SCARCITY MINDSET: THE FEAR OF NEVER HAVING ENOUGH

This is the belief that there's never enough. Never enough clients, never enough money, never enough time. When you operate from a scarcity mindset, you might find yourself constantly worrying about where the next client or pay check is coming from. This fear can drive you to make decisions based on lack rather than abundance.

For example, you might underprice your services because you're afraid clients won't pay more, or you might avoid investing in new tools, products or training because you're worried about spending money. The problem with this mindset is that it creates a self-fulfilling prophecy. By focusing on what you lack, you inadvertently attract more scarcity into your life and business.

How to Overcome It:

To overcome a scarcity mindset, start by shifting your focus from what you don't have to what you *do* have. Practise gratitude for the clients, skills and resources you already have. Set intentions based on abundance, such as, "I attract clients who value and pay for my skills," and remind yourself regularly that there are plenty to go around. It is also helpful to review your pricing structure to ensure you're charging what you should for your services. Clients who see your value will pay for it.

2. FEAR OF WEALTH:
THE BELIEF THAT MONEY WILL CHANGE YOU

Another common block is the fear of wealth, which stems from the belief that having a lot of money will change you for the worse. You might worry that earning more money will make you greedy, or that it will alienate you from friends and family. This fear can cause you to unconsciously sabotage your own success, keeping your income lower than it could be.

In the beauty industry, where you're often directly involved in client care and services, this fear might manifest as a reluctance to expand your business or raise your prices because you don't want to seem 'money-hungry' or out of touch with your clients.

How to Overcome It:

To overcome the fear of wealth, reframe your beliefs about money. Money is a tool. It doesn't change who you are: it amplifies the qualities you already have. If you're a generous and kind person, having more money will allow you to be more generous and make a bigger impact. Focus on the positive ways that increased income can enhance your life and your ability to serve others, whether through offering better services, supporting your community or achieving personal goals.

3. IMPOSTER SYNDROME: DOUBTING YOUR WORTH

Imposter syndrome is the feeling that you're not truly qualified, that you don't deserve your success, or that you're somehow 'faking it'. It is a common mindset block, especially for business owners just starting out or stepping into new levels of success. This can lead to under-pricing your services, overworking yourself to prove your worth, or hesitating to take on new opportunities because you fear you're not good enough.

Imposter syndrome might show up as doubting your skills, questioning your pricing, or feeling like you need to offer discounts or freebies to attract clients. It can also cause you to compare yourself to others in the industry, leading to feelings of inadequacy.

How to Overcome It:

To get over imposter syndrome, start by acknowledging your achievements and the value you bring to your clients. Keep a record of positive client feedback and personal milestones to remind yourself of what you can do. Surround yourself with supportive people or mentors who offer encouragement and lift you up. Everyone feels like an imposter at times, but push through those doubts and recognise that you are deserving of your success.

4. MONEY GUILT: THE DISCOMFORT OF EARNING MORE

Money guilt occurs when you feel uncomfortable about making more money, especially if you've surpassed what you thought was possible or what others around you are earning. You might feel like you don't deserve the money or that you should be doing more to help others with it. This guilt can lead to self-sabotage, such as giving away your earnings, undercharging, or overworking to 'earn' the money you've already made.

Money guilt might make you hesitant to raise your prices, even when your skills and services justify it. You might also feel uncomfortable with the idea of charging for consultations or premium services, or retailing, fearing that it's unfair to clients.

How to Overcome It:

Overcoming money guilt starts with recognising that your income is a reflection of the value you provide. It is okay to be paid well for your experience, hard work and the results you deliver to your clients. If you find yourself feeling guilty about your earnings, consider how you can use your financial success to support causes you care about or to improve your business and services. This can help you view money as a positive force for change rather than something to feel guilty about.

5. FEAR OF FINANCIAL RESPONSIBILITY: AVOIDING MONEY MANAGEMENT

Some business owners shy away from managing their finances because they fear making mistakes or they feel overwhelmed by the responsibility. This can lead to disorganisation, missed opportunities and even financial trouble. If you avoid your bank statements, delay charging no-shows or put off paying tax, this fear might be holding you back.

Avoiding financial responsibility can result in missed revenue opportunities, difficulty tracking expenses or a reluctance to invest in business growth.

How to Overcome It:

Face the fear of financial responsibility head-on by educating yourself on the basics of money knowledge and organisation. There are plenty of resources available, from online courses to books. Set up simple systems to track your income and expenses. Schedule regular financial check-ins to stay on top of your business's money. Managing your finances doesn't have to be complicated, and taking control of this part of your business will give you greater confidence and peace of mind.

These common money mindset blocks can create huge barriers to your success as a beauty business owner. Whether it's a scarcity mindset, fear of wealth, imposter syndrome, money guilt, or fear of financial responsibility, these blocks can prevent you from reaching your full potential. The good news is that by recognising these blocks and taking proactive steps to address them, you can change your relationship with money.

TRANSFORMING YOUR MONEY MINDSET

Now that you know about the common money mindset blocks, it's time to take action and start transforming your relationship with money. Shifting from a limiting mindset to one of abundance can make a big difference in your business and personal life.

The first step in changing your money mindset is to release the limiting beliefs that have been holding you back. These beliefs often come from under the surface, influencing your decisions without you even knowing. To start changing them, you need to bring them to light and challenge their truth.

How to recognise limiting beliefs:

- Self-reflection. Take time to reflect on your thoughts and feelings about money. When you think about pricing your services, making investments or spending money, what thoughts come up? Do you feel fear, guilt or anxiety? Write down any negative thoughts or patterns you notice.

- Journalling. Explore your beliefs about money by writing about them. Ask yourself questions like, "What do I believe about money?" or, "Why do I think I can't earn more?" Writing down your thoughts can help you uncover deeply ingrained beliefs that you need to address.

- Seek feedback. Sometimes, we're all too close to our own thoughts to see them clearly. Talking to a trusted mentor, coach or even a close friend can provide valuable insights into your money mindset. They might help you identify beliefs you didn't know were holding you back.

How to release limiting beliefs:

- Challenge the belief. Once you've identified a limiting belief, ask yourself if it's really true. For example, if you believe it when you say, "I'm not good with money," challenge that thought by reflecting on times when you've successfully managed your money, even in small ways.

- Replace the belief. After challenging a limiting belief, replace it with a more empowering one. If you've been thinking, "I can't charge that much," replace it with, "I provide valuable services and clients are happy to pay for them." Repeat these positive affirmations regularly to reinforce your new beliefs.

- Practise mindfulness. Pay attention to your thoughts and feelings about money as they arise. When you catch yourself falling back into old patterns of negative thinking, consciously choose to shift your mindset. Mindfulness can help you stay aware and make more intentional choices.

HAVING AN ABUNDANCE MINDSET

Moving from a scarcity mindset to an abundance mindset is a powerful shift that can open up new opportunities for growth in your beauty, hair or aesthetic business. An abundance mindset is rooted in the belief that there is more than enough to go around – more than enough clients, money, success and opportunities.

How to enact an abundance mindset:

- Gratitude practice. Start each day by reflecting on what you're grateful for. Gratitude shifts your focus from what you lack to what you already have, creating a foundation for an abundance mindset. Consider keeping a gratitude journal where you write down three things you're thankful for each day, especially related to your business.

- Affirmations. Use positive affirmations to reinforce your abundance mindset. Phrases like, "I attract clients who value and pay for my services," or, "Money flows to me easily and freely," can help reprogramme your mind to expect abundance.

- Visualisation. Take a few minutes each day to visualise your goals as if they've already been achieved. Picture your business growing, with a steady stream of clients, financial success and personal fulfilment. Visualisation helps you align your actions with your desired outcomes. I like doing this one in the morning when I'm in the shower.

- Focus on giving. An abundance mindset isn't only about receiving; it's also about giving. When you give freely, whether it's your time, expertise or even money, you reinforce the belief that there is plenty to go around. Consider ways you can give back, such as offering a free event to your community or mentoring a younger stylist.

BUILDING A HEALTHY RELATIONSHIP WITH MONEY

To truly transform your money mindset, it's a must to build a healthy, balanced relationship with money. This means viewing money not as something to be feared or avoided, but as a tool that can help you achieve your goals and create the life and business you dream of.

Steps to build a healthy relationship with money:

- Budget with purpose. Create a budget that aligns with your goals and values. Instead of viewing a budget as a tie, see it as a way to direct your tools toward what matters most to you, whether that's investing in your business, saving for the future or just enjoying life.

- Celebrate financial wins. Take time to celebrate your financial successes, no matter how small. Whether it's hitting a monthly revenue goal, paying off a debt or saving up for your favourite handbag, acknowledge these wins to help you create a positive relationship with money.

- Separate personal and business finances. If you haven't already, make sure your personal and business finances are separate. This not only makes managing your money easier but helps you view your business finances more objectively, reducing emotional attachment.

- Educate yourself. The more you understand about money, the more confident you'll feel in managing it. Take time to learn about financial topics relevant to your business, such as cash flow, pricing strategies and tax options. Knowledge is power when it comes to building a healthy money mindset.

SETTING FINANCIAL GOALS ALIGNED WITH YOUR VALUES

When your goals are aligned with your values and vision for your business, they become powerful motivators that guide your decisions and actions.

How to set financial goals:

- Identify your priorities. Start by identifying what's most important to you in your business and personal life. Do you want to expand your salon, invest in continuing education, start a training academy or achieve a better work-life balance? Your financial goals should reflect these priorities.

- Make goals specific and measurable. Instead of setting vague goals like 'make more money', be specific. For example: "Increase monthly revenue by twenty percent within the next six months," or "Save £10,000 for a salon renovation by the end of the year." Specific goals give you a clear target to aim for and make it easier to track your progress.

- Break down big goals. Large financial goals can feel overwhelming, so break them down into smaller, manageable steps. If your goal is to save £10,000 for a renovation, figure out how much you need to save each month and what actions you can take to reach that amount.

- Review and adjust regularly. Your financial goals should be dynamic, reflecting changes in your business and life. Regularly review your goals and adjust them as needed. Celebrate milestones along the way and don't be afraid to pivot if your priorities change.

MONEY MINDSET AND BUSINESS SUCCESS

Now that you've begun changing your money mindset, it's time to look at how this new perspective can have a major impact on the success of your beauty, hair or aesthetic business. Your mindset about money influences every financial decision you make, from how you price your services to how you invest in your growth. Let's work our way through this together.

1. SETTING THE RIGHT PRICES FOR YOUR SERVICES

You can find one of the most direct impacts of your money mindset on your business in how you set your prices. Many beauty business owners struggle with pricing – I have this conversation with most of my clients. They often undercharge because they fear clients won't pay more… or because they doubt the value of their services… or because the salon down the road is cheaper. However, under-pricing not only undermines your worth but can lead to burnout, as you're forced to work more hours to make up for low prices.

How to set confident prices:

- Value-based pricing. Start by understanding the value you provide to your clients. Consider the skills, experience and high-quality products you bring to the table. Clients don't just pay for the service itself, they pay for the entire experience and the results you deliver. When you recognise the value you offer, it becomes easier to set prices that reflect it.

- Research the market. Look at what other businesses in your area with similar services charge. While you don't want to base your prices solely on what others are doing (as everyone has different overheads), this research can give you a sense of what clients are willing to pay in your market. If your services are unique or superior, don't be afraid to charge a premium.

- Test and adjust. Don't be afraid to test different pricing strategies. You might start with one price point and then adjust based on client feedback, demand and how the pricing aligns with your financial goals. It is okay to raise your prices as your business grows and your skills advance. I recommend doing a price increase at least every six months.

- Check your business outgoings. You need to know
  your break-even points as a service-based business.
  How much does it cost you per hour to open the doors?
  It could be costing you £30 an hour to open your salon
  or clinic. If you only charge £30 an hour for a treatment,
  you are only breaking even, not making any profit.

When you set your prices with confidence and align them with
the value you provide, you'll attract clients who appreciate your
services and are willing to pay for them. This, in turn, boosts
your revenue and allows you to invest more in your business
and in yourself.

2. INVESTING IN YOUR BUSINESS

Another critical part of business success is knowing when and
where to invest in your business. A scarcity mindset might
make you hesitant to spend money, even on things that could
help your business grow, like marketing, a business coach, new
equipment or advanced training. However, a positive money
mindset sees these expenditures as investments that can bring
you a return.

Smart investments for beauty businesses:

- Marketing. Effective marketing is essential for
  attracting new clients and growing your business.
  Whether it's upgrading your website, running
  targeted social media ads or investing in a professional
  photographer to showcase your work, spending money
  on marketing can lead to increased visibility and client
  bookings.

- Education and training. The beauty industry is always evolving, with new techniques, products and trends emerging regularly. Investing in continuing education not only keeps your skills sharp but also allows you to offer the latest services to your clients, setting you apart from your competitors.

- Investment in a business coach or mastermind. It is important to have someone to direct you, hold your hand in business and speed up your success. Running a business can be extremely lonely and having that person to help you build your business and point you in the right direction can help you stay accountable and speed up your growth.

- Tools and products. High-quality tools, machines and products are essential for delivering excellent results. Investing in the best materials enhances the client experience and shows your commitment to quality, which can justify higher prices.

When you view these expenses as investments rather than costs, you're more likely to make decisions that support the long-term growth and sustainability of your business. The goal is to spend money in ways that will return value to your business, whether through increased client satisfaction, higher revenue or improved efficiency.

3. MANAGING CASH FLOW WITH CONFIDENCE

Cash flow is the lifeblood of any business and managing it is a must for long-term success. A scarcity mindset might lead you to avoid looking at your finances regularly out of fear or anxiety, but this can lead to bigger problems down the line. A positive money mindset, on the other hand, encourages you to take control of your finances, allowing you to make informed decisions and plan for the future.

Strategies for better cash flow:

- Regular financial reviews. Schedule regular check-ins with your finances, such as weekly or monthly reviews. I always teach my clients to do CEO Sundays with me. Look at your income and expenses, and always put aside your tax and VAT. This practice helps you stay on top of your cash flow and avoid unpleasant surprises.
- Plan for seasonality. Many beauty businesses experience seasonal fluctuations in revenue. Plan ahead for slower periods by saving during busier times or offering special promotions to keep cash flow steady. Understanding the rhythms of your business can help you navigate these ups and downs a lot easier.
- Build an emergency fund. A financial cushion can provide peace of mind and protect your business from unexpected expenses. Aim to save a portion of your revenue each month until you have enough to cover at least three months' operating expenses.

By actively managing your cash flow, you can make more confident decisions about when to save and when to invest.

4. EMBRACING FINANCIAL RESPONSIBILITY

Taking control of your business's finances means embracing financial responsibility. This involves not only managing your cash flow but understanding the financial health of your business and making informed decisions that support your goals.

Key areas of financial responsibility:

- Budgeting. Create and stick to a budget that aligns with your business goals. A budget helps you manage your stock effectively and makes sure you spend money on the things that matter most.

- Tracking expenses. Keep track of all your business expenses, from product costs to utilities to marketing spend. Knowing where your money goes helps you see areas where you can cut costs or invest more.

- Setting financial goals. Make clear financial goals for your business, such as turnover targets, profit margins or savings goals. Regularly review your progress toward these goals and adjust as needed.

When you have financial responsibility, you gain a clearer picture of your business's financial health, which helps you to make decisions that support growth and success.

5. LEVERAGING YOUR MONEY MINDSET FOR GROWTH

Finally, a positive money mindset can be a powerful tool for driving business growth. When you believe in your ability to generate and manage money, you're more likely to take the necessary steps to grow your business, attract more clients and achieve your money goals.

Ways to leverage your money mindset for growth:

- Scaling your business. As your business grows, consider ways to scale, such as opening another location, expanding your service offerings or hiring more staff. A positive money mindset allows you to see these opportunities as achievable and worth pursuing.

- Networking and partnerships. Building relationships with other professionals in the beauty industry can open up new opportunities for growth. Whether it's collaborating on a special event, cross-promoting services or learning from each other's experiences, a positive money mindset encourages you to seek out and capitalise on these opportunities.

- Innovating and adapting. The beauty industry is constantly changing and staying ahead of trends is key to long-term success. A positive money mindset empowers you to invest in innovation, whether it's through new services, products or business models, helping you stay competitive and relevant.

By leveraging your money mindset, you can turn challenges into opportunities and drive your business toward greater success and financial freedom.

Your money mindset is not just a personal belief system; it's a powerful force that influences every aspect of your beauty business. From setting prices and investing in growth to managing cash flow and having financial responsibility, a positive money mindset empowers you to make confident, informed decisions that support your success. By transforming your relationship with money, you open the door to new opportunities, greater financial freedom and scaling your business.

CEO SUNDAYS

My clients know I love doing my numbers every week: my CEO Sundays. I used to do it every Monday morning, but I now do it on a Sunday night as I know I will have no distractions and I am set up for the week. The reasons I do my numbers every week rather than every month are, firstly, it's quicker and saves time, secondly, it keeps me on track with my numbers every week, and thirdly, it doesn't feel as much to transfer to my pots, making it more manageable.

I started doing this from day one of my first salon. Doing my accounts every week made me want to beat the previous week. It helped me see a pattern of when our quiet times and our busy times were. It helped me predict the future turnover of the business and ultimately gave me more control over what I was doing in the business and what I was spending my money on.

Now I do this with my clients. Every week we see what we made that week, what our profit margins were and transfer our money pots. The money pots can be for anything you feel you need to put aside. I always suggest at least a VAT pot, a tax pot and a savings pot. You can have as many pots as you like, depending on what your bank allows. Some banks actually call them pots, while with others you need to open savings accounts attached to your current accounts.

The reason we set up pots is so when bills come out (your VAT, for example), you know you have it there ready. It doesn't feel as much of a dent in your pocket when that horrible VAT return is due. None of us likes paying it, but we have to, and this is the easiest way I have found to manage it.

I have seen many business owners struggle and some even have to close their doors due to VAT. It is awfully sad. We blame the VAT, yes, and we don't understand why we have to pay it, and we imagine what our bank balances would look like if we didn't need to pay VAT. I say that all the time, but we struggle more with paying the VAT when we don't manage our money correctly and put it aside every week. For me, that's the first pot I transfer.

We can all stamp our feet and scream how much we hate it, but I suggest you try to see it as a huge success that your business turns over enough money that you are liable for VAT. If you charge correctly, making your prices reflect the VAT, you should be able to put aside the VAT easily each week even though it hurts.

Meet my client Abbie from HON Salon and Academy in Mountsorrel, Loughborough. She is part of my Growth Mastermind. She has a home-based nail salon and training academy. When Abbie started with me, she didn't know her numbers or pricing at all. Break-even points weren't even a thought and figures weren't looked at until she had to file her tax return.

Over my time working with Abbie, she started doing her numbers and her money pots every week. Instead of finding this a boring task like you might think, she actually found it exciting. We put money goals in place for her to hit every week and looked at how many clients she would need and how many courses she would need to book students on to hit this. When she hit her goals, we put new ones in place.

Before Abbie started with me, she was taking around £400 a week. Within her first month with me she was taking around £800-£1000 a week. Every month she messages me to celebrate her growing monthly income. Her success came down to understanding and knowing her numbers, making sure her pricing was correct and having her financial goals in place. I am so excited to see where Abbie goes next in her journey.

PRACTICAL EXERCISES TO IMPROVE YOUR MONEY MINDSET

Now that we've gone through the theory and you've heard real-life examples, it's time to take action. Let's see how you can work things into your daily life and create routines to help you improve your money mindset.

DAILY AFFIRMATIONS

Affirmations are powerful statements that help reprogramme your subconscious mind to align with your goals. By repeating positive affirmations every day, you can begin to shift your beliefs and attitudes about money.

Select a few affirmations that align with the money mindset you want to change.

 For example:

"I attract clients who value and pay for my services."

"Money flows to me easily and abundantly."

"I am worthy of financial success and abundance."

Take a few moments each morning or evening to say your affirmations out loud or to write them down. The more you practise, the more these positive statements will become ingrained in your thinking. As you say your affirmations, visualise the outcomes you desire. Picture yourself achieving your financial goals, feeling confident and empowered. Visualisation adds an extra layer of impact to your affirmations. This might all sound 'woo woo' but stay with me: it works.

I have compiled a list of affirmations for you to practise with: **www.kgbusinessmentor.com/book**

JOURNALLING FOR MONEY MINDSET

Journalling is a powerful tool for self-reflection and growth. It allows you to explore your thoughts and feelings about money, identify limiting beliefs and set intentions for the future.

Start by writing about your current beliefs and feelings about money. What comes to mind when you think about your finances? Are there any negative thoughts or fears that surface?

Write about the influences that shaped your money mindset – your childhood, cultural background and personal experiences. Understanding these influences can help you see where your beliefs come from and how they might be holding you back.

Use your journal to set clear intentions for your money mindset. For example: "I intend to embrace an abundance mindset and trust that money will flow to me as I provide value to my clients."

Journal regularly about your experiences and progress as you work on your money mindset. Celebrate your wins, no matter how small, and reflect on any challenges you encounter along the way. Lola-Rose and I journal every morning when we wake up to start our day right.

VISUALISATION EXERCISES

Visualisation is a technique used by many successful people to achieve their goals. By mentally rehearsing the outcomes you desire, you can create a strong belief in your ability to achieve them, which in turn influences your actions.

Dedicate five to ten minutes each day to visualising your financial goals and business success. Find a quiet space where you won't be disturbed. Imagine yourself achieving your goals in vivid detail. For example, visualise your beauty business growing, with a steady stream of clients, financial stability and the freedom to live the life you dream of.

As you visualise, engage all your senses. What does your successful business look like? How does it feel to achieve your financial goals? What sounds, smells or tastes are associated with your success? The more detailed your visualisation, the more powerful it will be.

As you visualise, focus on the emotions you'll feel when you achieve your goals. Joy, pride, confidence, security. These positive emotions help reinforce your belief in your ability to succeed.

SETTING AND REVIEWING FINANCIAL GOALS

Setting clear financial goals is essential for maintaining a positive money mindset and achieving long-term success. These goals give you a roadmap and help you stay focused on what matters most.

Start by identifying your short-term and long-term financial goals. These could include increasing your monthly revenue, saving for a major purchase, paying off debt or expanding your business.

Ensure your goals are specific and measurable. For example: "Increase monthly revenue by 20% in the next six months," or, "Save £5,000 for a business coach by the end of the year."

Break down larger goals into smaller, actionable steps. This makes them more manageable and allows you to track your progress along the way.

Set aside time each week to review your financial goals. Assess your progress, celebrate any milestones and make adjustments if necessary. Regular reviews help keep you accountable and motivated.

PRACTISING GRATITUDE FOR FINANCIAL ABUNDANCE

Gratitude is a powerful practice that shifts your focus from what you lack to what you already have. By practising gratitude, you reinforce an abundance mindset and attract more positive experiences into your life and business.

Each day, write down three things you're grateful for related to your finances or business. This could be anything from a new client booking to a recent financial win or simply having the resources to pursue your passion.

Take time to express gratitude to your clients for their business. Whether it's through a thank-you note, a special offer or a personal message, showing appreciation strengthens your relationships and fosters a positive energy in your business.

Periodically reflect on how far you've come in your financial journey. Acknowledge the progress you've made, the challenges you've overcome, and the abundance that has flowed into your life as a result of your hard work and positive mindset.

Remember, this journey is ongoing. As you continue to grow and scale your business and yourself, so will your relationship with money. Keep practising the strategies you've learned in this chapter, and don't hesitate to revisit the exercises whenever you need a boost. With a positive money mindset, there's no limit to what you can achieve in your business and beyond.

6

PERSONAL BRANDING: WHY PEOPLE BUY FROM PEOPLE

In today's world, personal branding is more important than ever. People buy from people. Even more than that, they buy from people they *like* and *trust*. How can you get the public to like you and buy into your services if they don't even know you?

This is where personal branding comes into play. Your brand is more than just your business: it's the entire essence of who you are and how you connect with people. And a huge part of personal branding is sharing your story. I often hear people say, "I don't have a story," or, "No one would be interested in me." But the truth is, we *all* have a story, no matter how big or small. And yes, people are interested in you; it's part of human nature to connect with others through shared experiences.

BUILDING MY BRAND THROUGH STORYTELLING

Let me share with you how my personal brand started and evolved. I left school at thirteen due to bullying, and when I opened my salon at nineteen with no qualifications, that itself was a story. The local media loved it. They shared my journey in newspapers and highlighted my challenges and achievements, framing my story around resilience and entrepreneurship. Headlines like *"Don't Let the Bullies Win"* and *"Teenage Entrepreneur Opens Business"* attracted attention and helped people see me as a fighter, someone worth supporting.

Over the years, these stories continued to resonate. People still remembered them and they chose KG Salon not just because of the services but because of the personal connection they felt to my journey. When you get off the tools in your business, this is why people still come, even though you might not be doing the treatments. It is also why they stay with a brand even if their favourite therapists leave over time.

When social media arrived, I started to share more of my life online. I showed the real side of running a business – the good, the bad and the challenging. This authenticity deepened my connection with my audience. I was attracting not just clients but a network of people who related to me, who felt inspired by my resilience, and who wanted to see me succeed. This network grew even further as I won awards and began speaking at schools and colleges, which added to my credibility.

Fast-forward to my time as a single mum, building my business while raising my daughter, Lola-Rose, and travelling the world. Headlines like *"Jet-Set Mum: I Quit School at 13 with No GCSEs, Now My Beauty Business Earns Me £600k a Year"* in *The Sun* might make me cringe, but they also connected with people. These stories led to more clients, more students, and ultimately, more revenue for my businesses.

Teenage entrepreneur opens businesses

A 19-YEAR-OLD Luton model, who left school early due to incessant bullying, has opened four businesses under one roof in Barton.

Katie Godfrey, of Kingsdown Avenue, dropped out of Icknield High School aged 13, leaving her with no GCSEs.

But the lack of qualifications has not stopped the budding entrepreneur, who is now the owner of KG Model Management, KG Tanning, KG Nails and KG Studios in Bedford Road.

The salon is a one-stop shop for those in need of pampering and promoting themselves as it houses a tanning salon, nail technicians, model agency and photographic studio.

Katie, who has been a model for six years and ran KG Model Management from home for a year before opening the salon, said: "I hated school so much because of the bullying. I've had a model agency for a year now, but in a premises, just a model agency was not going to make enough money.

"I always wanted a tanning salon so I thought I'd get a building big enough to get all four businesses in it. We rent the photograph-

BUSINESS MINDED: Katie Godfrey has opened four businesses under one roof aged just 19

ic studio out if I haven't got models in it."

And despite the credit crunch, the new business venture is bound to be a success with Katie's positive thinking.

Katie said: "I'm not going to let it stop me. Every woman wants to

be pampered and they've always got £20 to get their nails done."

Call the salon on 01582 883611.

>> Don't miss the Business Monthly supplement free inside next Wednesday's issues of our sister papers The Luton News and Dunstable Gazette.

Katie featured in local press.

Fabulous > Parenting

JET SET MUM I quit school at 13 with no GCSEs – now my business earns me £600k a year, I love jetting off to Dubai with my kid

The Sun feature Katies story.

(https://www.thesun.co.uk/fabulous/23094030/single-mum-no-gcses-businesses-trips-kid/)

Now, let's break down how you can find your own personal brand, build your unique story and share it with the world to build your business.

1. FINDING YOUR PERSONAL BRAND: WHO ARE YOU BEYOND THE BUSINESS?

Your personal brand is essentially the 'you' behind your business. It is the qualities, values and experiences that make you unique and memorable. So, ask yourself: *What makes you different from everyone else?* What's your unique angle or story that would connect with your ideal client?

Start by figuring out your core values and what drives you. Your values shape your approach to business and sharing them will help you attract clients who resonate with those same values. Make a list of your top five values. Are you passionate about quality, empowerment, creativity or community? Understanding these values will help you shape the tone and message of your brand.

Your unique skills, strengths and quirks are part of what sets you apart. Maybe you're particularly good at connecting with clients on a personal level, or you're known for being meticulous with your services. Identify these aspects of yourself and think about how they contribute to your business. List your top three strengths and think about how they impact your business. Consider including these qualities in your brand message so clients see the value in what makes you different.

Think about experiences that have shaped who you are. Did you overcome challenges to build your business? Have you made sacrifices to pursue your passion? Did you have a tough upbringing? Are you a mum running a business? These experiences not only make you relatable, but they also add depth to your brand. For example, if you grew up in a small town with limited growth but managed to build a successful business, share that story. People love to support those who've overcome obstacles and worked hard to succeed.

2. CREATING YOUR STORY: SHARING THE MOMENTS THAT MATTER

Once you have a better understanding of who you are and what makes you unique, it's time to create your story. Your story is more than a biography, it's the journey that got you where you are today. It is not about perfection but authenticity, resilience and growth. The key is to share moments that reveal who you are, what you care about and why you're passionate about what you do.

Being vulnerable and sharing the challenges you've faced builds trust with your audience. People want to connect with someone real, not someone who pretends everything is always perfect. Don't be afraid to share the struggles, the lessons learned and even the mistakes made along the way. When I shared my story of leaving school early due to bullying, people connected with me on a personal level. I wasn't just a business owner, I was someone who had faced hardship and pushed through.

Highlighting the challenges you've faced and how you've overcome them not only makes you relatable but positions you as a role model. It shows that you didn't have an easy path but chose to persevere, which can inspire others who may face their own struggles. For example, if you faced financial difficulties starting out but managed to build a successful business, share that. Explain the tough times and how they made you stronger or helped you create better systems.

While sharing struggles is essential, don't forget to celebrate your successes as well. Whether it's winning an award, reaching a business milestone or helping a client in a significant way, these wins are part of your story. They show your audience that hard work pays off and builds credibility. When I won the Eyelash Technician of the Year award and shared it on social media, it validated my work and helped people see me as a credible expert in my field… but also helped me sell out my eyelash training courses at KG Professional.

3. GETTING YOUR BRAND OUT THERE: BUILDING AND SHARING YOUR PERSONAL BRAND

Now that you've defined your brand and built your story, it's time to put it out there. Visibility is key to building trust and attracting clients. The more people know about you, the more they'll feel connected to you and the more likely they are to choose your business over others.

Social media is one of the most powerful tools for sharing your personal brand. Consistently post content that reflects who you are, your values and your journey. Share behind-the-scenes moments, client transformations and even day-to-day life updates. Use platforms like Instagram Stories and Facebook Lives to connect with your audience in real time. This gives followers a glimpse into your personality and creates a feeling of authenticity. Stories are a great way to start as they don't need to be perfect and disappear in twenty-four hours. You could share short videos of your daily routine, your thoughts on industry trends or even the struggles you face. This keeps your followers engaged and helps build a personal connection.

Your personal brand isn't just about your online presence. Attend industry events, join local business groups and network with other professionals. Building face-to-face relationships with people in your community or industry helps reinforce your brand.

Attend events like beauty events and local entrepreneur meetups, or even host your own workshops. These face-to-face interactions allow people to experience your personality and brand firsthand. Hosting a workshop at a local college or attending a beauty show and sharing your journey with others not only builds credibility but spreads your brand through word of mouth.

You can boost your personal brand significantly by getting your story featured in the media. A well-told story in the media not only builds credibility but also reaches a wider audience. I have managed to do this over one hundred times over the years. Reach out to local newspapers, industry magazines, online publications or beauty industry websites to share your story. Pitch your story with an angle that makes it unique or newsworthy, such as overcoming adversity or building a successful business from scratch.

When I was featured in *The Sun* with headlines like *"I Left School with No GCSEs, Now My Beauty Business Rakes in £500k a Year"* it helped me gain recognition beyond my local network. Don't be afraid to let your story go big.

Email marketing is still one of the most effective ways to build connections and loyalty. Use your email list to share personal stories, business updates and insights into your life. This helps clients and followers feel like part of your journey. Mix your emails up to share a personal story, business updates and new services or products. Include value-driven content that offers tips or advice to your audience.

My email list is a place where I can share more in-depth stories and updates with my audience. I've found that the more I open up in emails, the more responses I get from readers who feel inspired by or connected to my journey. Emails are a direct line to your audience, allowing you to nurture relationships with clients who are already invested in you and your brand. Over time, this builds loyalty and keeps your business at the forefront of their minds.

4. BUILDING A COHESIVE PERSONAL BRAND IMAGE

Your personal brand isn't only what you say; it's also how you present yourself visually. From the way you dress to the colours and design on your social media feeds, everything contributes to your brand image. When you are consistent across your online and offline presence, you will strengthen people's recognition of you and make it easier for clients to connect with your brand. I recommend you have professional headshots done and use the same one across everything you do: your display image, your website and any magazine articles. This keeps you recognisable.

As part of your brand, your appearance should reflect the image you want to convey to clients. Think about how you want clients to perceive you. If your brand is about natural beauty, for example, consider a more neutral, understated look. If you're known for bold, colourful styles, let your wardrobe and appearance reflect that. Whether your look is polished and professional or trendy and creative, consistency in how you present yourself reinforces the brand's message and builds trust.

Your visual identity includes the colours, fonts, logo and overall style you use in everything from social media posts to emails. This visual cohesion builds trust and helps your audience recognise your brand instantly. Choose a colour palette, fonts and design elements that align with your brand's personality. For example, a beauty business with a luxurious feel might use soft pastels, while a more vibrant, energetic brand might use bright colours. A nail technician I worked with built her brand around a soft blush pink and metallic gold palette, representing elegance and femininity. She used these colours on her website, price lists and social media, creating a seamless and recognisable look.

Your digital presence should consistently reflect your brand's tone and personality. This doesn't mean you need to share every aspect of your life, but showcasing specific parts of your journey and personality will build a strong and authentic brand.

Decide on the 'pillars' of your personal brand. These could be topics you always discuss, such as your business journey, beauty tips or motivational advice. These pillars help clients understand what to expect from you and why they should keep coming back. For example, a particular wellness coach's online persona includes her passion for fitness, nutrition and mental health tips. Her content regularly shows glimpses of her lifestyle, workouts and wellness routines, which creates a well-rounded, authentic brand that resonates with her followers.

5. CONNECTING WITH YOUR AUDIENCE THROUGH PERSONAL BRAND STORYTELLING

Telling your story effectively and authentically is central to building a strong personal brand. Clients resonate with stories because they're relatable and create an emotional bond. Crafting a real story about who you are and what you stand for will set you apart from competitors.

An engaging story often follows a basic structure: background, challenges faced, the 'aha' moment and the outcome. This structure allows people to follow your journey and connect with the highs and lows, making your brand relatable and memorable. My story arc includes leaving school early, facing challenges as a young entrepreneur, finding success through resilience, through to navigating running a business with babies. Each part adds to my brand's message that with determination, anyone can build the life they want. Write down your personal story in a few key points following the story arc. Start with your background, introduce the challenges, and describe how you overcame them. End with where you are now and what you're passionate about going forward.

With client permission, share their stories and results as well as your own story. This can be through testimonials, before-and-after photos, or even guest posts where they share their experiences with your business. Videos are also powerful. Sharing your clients' success stories adds depth to your brand and shows the real impact of your work. It helps potential clients see themselves in the story and motivates them to seek out your services.

A lash artist I work with regularly shares before-and-after photos of clients with brief stories about how the lashes helped boost their confidence. These mini client stories resonate with her audience, who can see the transformative power of her work. This gets her more bookings.

People love to see the process behind your services and products. Sharing behind-the-scenes content makes your brand feel real and transparent, giving your audience an insider's view of your work and life. Use stories or posts to show moments from your day, like setting up a treatment area, preparing products or even tidying up after a busy day. This glimpse into your routine builds relatability and trust.

A particular hair salon owner uses Instagram Stories to show the hustle of a fully booked Saturday, from setting up stations to celebrating with the team after a successful day. These snippets make followers feel part of the journey and highlight the dedication behind every appointment.

6. EXPANDING YOUR REACH AND BUILDING YOUR COMMUNITY

Once your brand is established, building a community around it can amplify your reach. A loyal community means more clients and more people who will promote your business through word-of-mouth and referrals. Engagement builds loyalty. Commenting on posts, responding to messages and creating interactive content makes followers feel valued and invested in your journey.

Host Q&A sessions, polls or 'Ask Me Anything' sessions so that clients can connect with you directly. Dedicate time to respond to comments and messages. It really bugs me when people don't reply to comments. Someone has taken the time to comment on your post, which has helped your post stay visible for a little longer... at least comment back.

Organising events like shopping events or workshops helps put a face to your brand, creating deeper connections with clients. These interactions not only strengthen brand loyalty but provide clients with value beyond the services you offer.

Consider building an online group for clients, such as a Facebook group. This allows clients to interact with each other and build connections with your brand at the same time. It could be a private group where you share exclusive tips, answer questions or give sneak peeks into new services and products. The feeling of exclusivity makes clients feel part of something special.

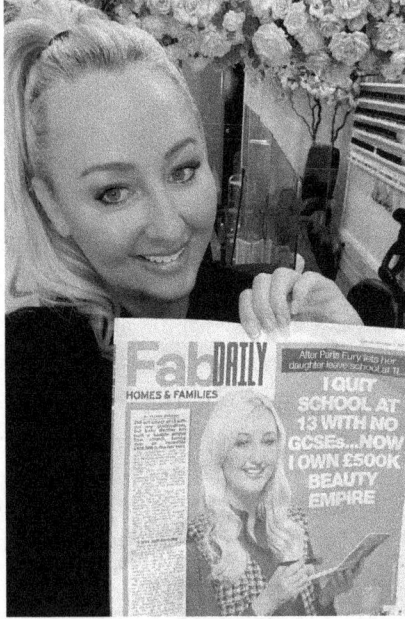

Katie published in The Sun, Fab Daily

(https://www.thesun.co.uk/fabulous/16594038/school-no-gcses-beauty-business-bossing-it/)

ADJUST YOUR CONTENT BASED ON ENGAGEMENT

Track the performance of your content across platforms. You can use social media analytics tools to evaluate engagement rates. Do certain types of post receive more likes, comments and shares? Adjusting your content strategy to focus on what resonates will keep your brand relevant. Regularly update your content plan to reflect the topics, tones or styles your audience engages with most. I am sure you will find that the content you put out that shows more of you, your personality and your personal brand will get the most love. Test it and give it a go.

Building a personal brand isn't a quick fix; it's a long-term investment and your brand will evolve over time, just as you do. It is not about creating a perfect image but about sharing your authentic self and showing the values that guide you in business and in life. When you're authentic and consistent, you'll attract clients who value what you offer and are loyal to your business. You don't have to change who you are in order to appeal to everyone. Focus on being true to yourself and your story, and you'll build a brand that grows with you. As you continue this journey, remember that a strong personal brand doesn't just create more bookings, it builds a community of clients who believe in your mission, support your vision and see the person behind the business. And that, ultimately, is what drives long-lasting success.

7

CREATE A TEAM: THE ULTIMATE FREEDOM

Wait. Don't let the word 'team' put you off and make you skip this chapter. Let's get educated on this subject for your future.

Creating a team is the number one thing I see salons and clinics going about the wrong way. It is also one of the subjects people are most uneducated on.

When you read this chapter you might think, "Oh my gosh, I'm doing this all wrong." Don't worry: you can correct whatever you are currently doing in your business. This isn't a call-out of those who are not doing it right. It purely is because I want you to do everything right to have the business you want and desire.

When it comes to building a team, there is only one real way to do this. There are other options that allow you to have people working within the business. But a *real* team... there is just one way. In this chapter, I will break down the options within the industry and explain how they work. Then you can decide which way is best for your business. There are also legal requirements when you create a team and I hope to save you from the consequences of not following the requirements just because you weren't aware.

I know for a fact that I would never be where I am in my career without building a team. I would never have had the freedom to travel the world while still earning money without a team. Sounds like a dream, right? But I will not sugar-coat it; it's not for everyone. Managing other human beings is not easy, and I haven't found anyone who says it is. I love having a team, but it took me years to become a leader. I had to be able to recruit well, set boundaries, and not have the urge to be liked and be everyone's friend. This was hard because in our industry, a lot of us are natural people pleasers. You need to develop that balance of being a good boss and developing their careers but not getting too close to the team personally. This protects you and them. I hear all the time, "We are like a family," when people talk about their teams. It is lovely they are close, but to me, this screams a lack of boundaries and someone is going to get hurt.

Building a team is not for you if you really don't want to manage anyone, or if you want to stay doing the treatments yourself and cap your earnings in the treatment room. Let me stress, this isn't a bad thing. As I said, having a team isn't for everyone, and we must all stay on our own path. You can make extra money in other ways like digital products, training, or property. But if you want to earn more from your salon or clinic, then you need to build a team. You might not be ready for this right now. You might feel in the future this is what you would like to do, as our wishes and ambitions can change all the time. At least you will have the knowledge of what is involved.

I also hear all the time that you are so busy with clients that you can't work on the business. You have no time to stay consistent with social media or other forms of marketing. You don't know your numbers or how much the business brings in. If you were to go on holiday, you'd be rushed off your feet with back-to-back clients before your holiday, then when you came back, you'd wonder what the point of going away was. You might even end up getting poorly on holiday as your body finally stops and goes into protection mode. To top it off, you wouldn't earn anything while you took this holiday because when you stop, the business stops.

Now don't hate me, but if the business stops earning when you stop working, you don't have a business; you're self-employed. If you take a holiday or a break and you stop earning because you aren't doing clients, you are self-employed. A business can carry on without you working in it physically day to day; you have a team working and it is scalable. There is a difference.

There isn't a right or wrong when it comes to the type of business model you choose regarding creating a team as long as you do it correctly, whether you use self-employed contractors to help you or an employed team. You must always think about what you want from your business and that will help you decide which way to go. Then you must build a team or delegate around what that looks like.

Maybe you want to have multiple businesses or freedom from your salon because right now you feel trapped doing clients all the time. You might start hating the salon because you have zero time, are always shattered, and clients moan if you take time off work. Maybe you love doing your clients, but you would love it even more if you could reduce your days to spend time with your family and be really present with them. Maybe you're thinking of having a baby or are currently pregnant and your business will have to go on hold. You hope and pray that you'll still even have a business after the baby is here.

If any of the above sounds like you, you're ready to start building a team.

I started building a team by employing people six months into opening my salon. I was nineteen years old and thought no one would take me seriously. I didn't even know how to interview; no one really teaches this stuff, do they? This was in 2009, and can you believe I put the ad in the local newspaper? That's how you advertised a job back then! Now I would say your go-to places for job advertisements are Indeed and social media.

Some amazing therapists I employed in those early days stayed with me for years. Others were not my greatest recruits. My top tips for recruiting are as follows:

HIRE SLOW, FIRE FAST

I use this phrase a lot with my clients.

Many people 'panic hire'. They hire quickly, perhaps someone with experience but who doesn't necessarily fit in with your salon culture.

One bad egg in the team can create a whole lot of bad energy, vibes and loss of other good staff members. I would normally suggest you go for personality and your gut feeling. You can't teach someone to have a personality, but you can teach them treatments. Not everyone is a unicorn at learning hair, beauty and aesthetics, which is why you also have a probationary period to make sure they are progressing and you are happy with their treatments.

ALWAYS DO A TRADE TEST

Please do a trade test with everyone. It doesn't matter if an applicant has worked in top spas across the country or worked on your favourite celebrity.

Some people interview extremely well. You do the trade test thinking they will be incredible, and you can't even believe it's the same person. Wax flying everywhere, a shaking mess, or even close to waxing a brow off! Honestly, I can't stress how important it is to have trade tests, ideally on multiple services.

DO THEY BADMOUTH THEIR OLD BOSS?

I can't deal with this one. From experience, I now stay well clear of anyone who does this, whether they have genuine reasons or not. I completely understand some bosses out there are horrible. I haven't personally had a boss, but I have heard horror stories from friends and family. But if you're interviewing someone and they talk badly of their boss or start telling you any gossip from their current workplace, see this as a massive warning sign not to employ them.

CRACKING THE SALON OWNER CODE

Over time, I recruited a team. It does take time; you don't want to take everyone on at the same time. Employ one person, wait until they are roughly eighty percent booked up, and then recruit the next person.

What I noticed was that even though I had this team, everyone still wanted me. I was the busiest therapist in the salon and I was by far the biggest earner. I can almost guarantee that any salon owner who's still doing treatments can resonate with this. You are busy while the staff have gaps. The clients choose you over anyone else. And even worse, you're scared your clients will go to the salon down the road if you hand them over to someone else.

I had this fear when I found out I was pregnant. *Holy crap, I thought, what am I going to do?* At the time, I was running two salons – my first beauty salon and a hairdresser's. Not to mention a busy training academy and product range. Within the beauty salon, I was the biggest earner and busy with clients all the time. I was also the only one in the salon who did lashes to a high standard, and this brought in most of our income alongside nail treatments.

I had to set a plan, put my CEO head on, and somehow get off this salon floor. I was so nervous about it. I needed to still earn the same without doing clients *and* keep everyone happy, before this baby came along. I felt guilty about handing my clients to somebody else to begin with. They had been with me for years, had been so loyal and now I was passing them over. But I knew I had to do this process. And I did it! Within three months of being pregnant, I was off the salon floor, kept every client in the business, and was overseeing how this was all going to work.

How, you're asking? I will give you a quick lowdown on my process.

I set a date by which I wanted to step away and not do clients anymore. I suggest putting in the diary the date you would love to stop doing clients or to cut down your days. This way you know it's happening and you can make all your planning work around this date. I recommend around three to six months for this process to happen, although I did it within ten weeks.

I got my team on board with my plan and did intense training with them. This was crucial. My staff were good at their jobs, but with me being the owner and the main therapist, they never had their time to shine. I made sure they had extra training in all the treatment areas they carried out. If they weren't trained in a treatment, I trained them up so there was no treatment that couldn't be done without me there. I held a team meeting about this whole process and the reasons I was stepping away. Obviously, it was to have my baby, but also so I could grow the business more. If the business grew, they could grow as therapists, pay rises could be more regular, and more treatments and products could be brought in. They saw the benefits of the growth of the business too, which was really important. You need your staff to come on board and support the stepping-out process you are doing.

I did a handover process over a period of time with my clients, warming them up each step of the way to who they were going to next for their treatments. This was the most important step and I didn't lose one single client. As soon as you have had that team meeting with your staff and got them on board, let your clients know. Tell them the reason you are stepping away, and its okay to be raw and open with them so they understand. If it's because you are burned out trying to do clients and run the business, tell them that. Explain why you have chosen the therapist or stylist you have to look after them and also explain that you are still around. If there are any problems, they can still raise them with you. Let the clients know in advance so they still have a few appointments with you as a handover process to reassure them. You can even get them to meet whoever is going to do their treatments in future.

It takes a lot of reassurance, communication and strict boundaries to make it happen. But it definitely can happen if you want it enough. And guess what? Once I stepped out of the salon and stopped doing clients, my salon and my brand just grew and grew as I had time to work on the business. I had the time to look at the company as a whole and work on improving what I couldn't see before because I was so head down with clients.

THE STACKING EFFECT

You might have a mental block around why you would hand over your clients and pay someone else a wage when you can do it yourself. You must see it as a stacking effect. You can only bring in so much income yourself and you are limited to a certain number of hours a day or week. Even if you want to stay on the salon or clinic floor, imagine if there were two of you bringing in what you bring in. Or three. Or four of you all doing clients. This is how your income stacks.

Let's use some basic numbers as an example. If you bring in £50 an hour and then you take on someone and they also bring you in £50 an hour, your business is now taking £100 an hour. Yes, minus their wages and overall expenses but that's more than you can take on your own. If there are four of you all bringing in £50 an hour, your business now takes £200 per hour.

Let me introduce you to Amy. She owns Bellissima Beauty and Aesthetics in Surrey. We started working together back in November 2020, when she was making around £3,000 a month in her salon with two self-employed girls, which was amazing. However, I knew she could achieve much more if she grew the business. Amy implemented everything I taught her, and before long, she took on an employed staff member and was hitting £7,000 a month. She then hired another staff member, making three of them there in total, and within two years, she was bringing in £25,000 a month. Let me repeat that: from £3,000 a month to £25,000 a month – how incredible is that? Amy also stepped out of the salon herself while the business generated this income. She had to reconsider her pricing, marketing and the treatments she offered to achieve this figure. But she wouldn't have been able to grow the business to this extent without the team… an *employed* team. Amy has now moved to a bigger premises and is taking on more staff. So you can only imagine the growth she will experience next.

EMPLOYMENT VERSUS SELF-EMPLOYMENT

Let's break down employment and self-employment when it comes to building a team. This is where I see things go wrong within our industry. This isn't because salon and clinic owners know they are doing it wrong and choose to ignore it. It is usually because there isn't much education on this subject, and we all tend to follow what others are doing.

By now, you will know if you are currently doing things wrong and need to change your setup, or how you want to build a team in the future, depending on your business plans. If you're doing things right currently, give yourself a pat on the back, as you're in the minority.

SELF-EMPLOYMENT

Self-employment is a great business model if you:

- Don't want to build a brand.
- Don't want to step off the floor and stop doing treatments.
- Just want to take some pressure off financially.
- Have no interest in expanding.
- Don't want to sell the business in the future.
- Are quite happy letting others run their own businesses within yours.

- Want no control over what they do within your business.

Self-employed business models typically involve renting out space on a day rate or a percentage split. In a percentage split, the therapist/stylist takes perhaps forty percent of the clients they see and the salon owner takes the other sixty percent. However, if the therapist/stylist doesn't have a client, nobody gets paid. If you're currently doing a percentage split in your business, please stop, as you can get in trouble for 'employment in disguise'. You don't want that court battle on your hands. Day rates are the best route to go down if you want self-employment within your salon.

When setting a day rate, charge a good amount. This all depends on your business outgoings. Lots of people charge to help cover their rent, but you mustn't forget all the other bills you also need to cover. I have seen salon owners charge £20-£30 a day for a chair or room. That is extremely cheap and the salon is more than likely making a loss on that arrangement. Outgoings, the size of your premises and your location play a part in what you should charge to rent out space, but remember that you are running a business: you want to cover your overheads and make a profit, otherwise, there isn't any point.

You have taken the risk of setting up your business, invested a lot of money, decked out your premises, and spent countless late nights working. You need to understand your break-even points to ensure you're charging enough to cover the overheads to open your doors. This is another common mistake I see, especially because everyone looks around to see what other salons are doing. If a salon down the road is renting out space, then the other salon owner up the road rents out space. Over the years this business model has grown a lot, so others are jumping on board as they feel this is the way you build a team – which it isn't and is just a lack of education.

Self-employment is a good business model if you have space that you just want filled, helping to pay the bills with some left over. But you must see yourself as a landlord within your business. That's the easiest way to describe it. They pay you rent, come and go as they please, and completely work for themselves. You can't set rules regarding uniforms or opening times or ask them to join team meetings, as they aren't your team. They work for themselves. Their payments should go through their own payment processor and they need to cover their own insurance. Your income is capped as you can only earn from doing the treatments yourself and the rental space.

The plus side is, it doesn't affect you as the salon owner if they aren't busy, as they still need to pay you rent. You won't have to cover holiday pay, maternity pay or taxes for them. However, if you want control over your business and unit and want to build a brand, I suggest you stay away from this business model as a salon/clinic owner. On the other hand, if the business is a concept in which many other businesses rent their own spaces, creating a hub/community with everyone under one roof paying rental space, this model works well.

EMPLOYMENT

Employment sounds scary, I know. It is definitely a respon- sibility. When you start employing, you also become a boss, which means stepping into a completely new role that you likely have no experience in. However, as much as it is scary and comes with responsibility, it is an incredible way to grow your business and gain freedom. I definitely wouldn't be where I am today without an employed team.

Let's go over the perks of employment:

- You can build a brand.
- You have full control over your business so you can apply rules on how you expect your staff to work within the business.
- You can mould and train team members to carry out treatments and provide customer experiences to suit you.
- You can set a culture within the salon/clinic.
- You can make a lot more money.
- You can step away and the business can run without you.

Ultimately, if you want your salon to become passive income one day, meaning you keep earning while you are not there or working, you want to employ a team. You can hand clients over to the team, knowing they are still your clients, within your business, with contracts in place to protect the business. If you hand over a client to someone self-employed, that client is no longer the business's; they are the self-employed person's client, which means they can take them to any location and you will lose the client you worked so hard to gain.

So, if you want that freedom lifestyle, to step back from the salon, or to one day sell the business, then employment is the way to make that happen. Yes, you have to pay their tax, and maternity pay if someone falls pregnant, and pay them even if there are no clients. But the bigger picture is so much more than this.

Let me introduce you to Laura from Laura Bell Salon. We started working together in 2020. Laura had a wonderful salon with a self-employed therapist and stylist, doing amazingly well, taking between £10,000 and £17,000 a month. But she was working every day on the salon floor and was totally exhausted. Being a natural entrepreneur, she also wanted more than the salon and started a product range and training academy. We had to get her off the salon floor for this to happen, which meant changing her business model and employing a team. Within three years, her salon was turning over £45,000 a month! She more than doubled her income and stepped out of the salon, giving her time to work on the business and her multiple other ventures. She wouldn't have been able to do this without a team. We are now working on her becoming a million-pound business. Who said there is no money in beauty?

Running a team is definitely the hardest part of having a business, though. I know some people who have tried it and hated managing people. It wasn't for them. The hardest part for many business owners is creating boundaries with the team. A lot of the time, in this industry, we are people pleasers. We want to be liked, so we want to be liked by our team. Of course, we do. But there is a difference between being liked by the team and becoming their best friends.

As soon as that line is blurred, it usually ends up with someone getting hurt. This is hard when you're working in the salon every day, as you all become close, share your day-to-day lives with each other and you become one of them. But when it comes time to pull someone up for a complaint or something you want to change, it's extremely hard to discipline that person because you're 'friends'. If they leave and hand in their notice, you will take it personally and end up getting hurt.

This was a significant lesson I learned in business. It took me years to really understand it. I have been hurt by staff members so many times I have lost count. Usually, it's by those you least expect. You grow tough skin over time, that's for sure. When someone left the salon, I would get really hurt too. I would think… How could they do that to me? I thought we were family. I thought they loved it here. Also, I told them so much about everything, I worried they would now tell others and not keep things confidential. I had trained them from the beginning and now they had left. I felt used. All sorts of thoughts would run through my mind.

This is where boundaries come into play, which help and protect you as the salon owner but also protect and help the employee too. You can be friendly with your team; you can be the best boss – I know I am. But always remember you are their boss. Keep relationships within work, hold back some of your personal life, keep contact within salon hours, do not meet up socially every week for dinner and drinks, hold team meetings and one-to-ones, and pull them up when there are issues with open communication, These points will help you maintain boundaries.

This also helps when people leave the business to either work somewhere else or start their own business. This is my thinking, which I hope will help you: You have helped them build a career, become better therapists or stylists, and they have made you money and helped your business while working for you. It is time for them to spread their wings and you have helped them on their journey. Everyone will leave at some point.

I love the fact that the girls who have left me to set up their own salons or work from home around their babies have gained the training and confidence to do that because of me, and I have been part of their journeys. No one can take that away from you as a salon owner. There is enough business for everyone and everyone also has their own ideal clients. Not all clients will want to come to you. People panic and feel like the industry is over-saturated, but it isn't. Be a good boss, leader and educator to your team. If you treat them with respect and have a good culture within the salon/clinic, they will usually reciprocate. A happy team stays with you for a long time.

WHEN IS THE RIGHT TIME TO BUILD A TEAM?

The easiest answer is when you're fully booked or turning away business. Staff will always be your biggest cost so keep payroll as low as you can while you build. Gain your first team member when you're turning away business *or* if you want to bring something into the business that you don't currently offer.

When I took on my first team member, I knew they had to be NVQ level 3 because I wasn't. I wanted my salon to offer all types of beauty treatments, something I wasn't qualified in nor did I want to be. I handled clients for the treatments I loved, mainly lashes, nails and hair extensions. My staff members would do these too, but also waxing, massages, facials, etc. I always recommend taking someone on part-time and getting them to build their columns and become busy. Then you can extend their hours or take on the next staff member.

If you are thinking you don't want a team *or* anyone self-employed, remember you can't be all things to all people. My bet is you're doing everything: the clients, the cleaning, the accounts, the social media, the marketing... the list goes on. Look at what you don't like doing or the areas that aren't your strong points and delegate those tasks. If you love doing treatments and don't want to think about putting down the tools, that's fine. But what can you get support on to help you avoid burnout or give you more time to do more clients? It might be delegating your bookkeeping or social media so you can concentrate on your clients. Building a team and a support network can be done in many ways.

Katie and her daughter Lola-Rose and son, Brodee holidaying in Dubai.

Katie and her family spent the summer in Bali
while the businesses were still running.

8

HOW TO LEAD AND MOTIVATE YOUR TEAM

The only thing that will give you true freedom while running a salon or clinic is building a team, but you also need to become a leader. A real CEO, I like to call it. This is separating your emotions from work and seeing this business as a business, rather than a job or an expensive hobby. You have a team, which means you need to lead them to be the best they can be, raise them as individuals and be able to keep them motivated long term. You are the leader, the person driving this business forward and leading the team to how you want them to be within the business. This takes time, practice and resilience. Oh, and lots of mistakes. I have made loads over the years, but they have made me into a better boss and leader.

This means things like being too close to the team and wanting to be their friend rather than 'boss', and not setting boundaries that then made things hard when it came to disciplinaries and even building the business.

If you don't lead correctly, you can stunt your own business growth and also your employee's. This doesn't mean you can't be friendly with your team; it is important that you are approachable with anything they wish to come to you for regarding the business or personal issues, but just because you can behave in a friendly manner, it doesn't mean being their friend. By 'friend', I mean going out and socialising outside of work and blurring the boundaries.

Keeping the boundaries clear also helps when it comes to delegating tasks to the team. As business owners we are naturally control freaks. I know I was, and it's taken me a long time to practise how let go of the business more, let go of that inner control freak and let the team take over. I had to start delegating small things to begin with and then do more and more. I would call myself the delegation queen now.

I remember being the one that had to do the stock ordering so it was always correct and I knew how much money I was spending. I had to be the one to open in the mornings to make sure everything was perfect before clients came in. And I had to close the salon in the evening to make sure the cash was put away and the salon was definitely locked up right and the alarm was on. I had to be the person who did my social media and email marketing because I couldn't imagine letting someone else do this who might make a mistake or do it not in line with my branding. How awful would that look?

Well, that was the mistake I was making: I was doing it all! As business owners we wear all the hats: problem solver, trainer, boss, friend, accountant, advisor, creator, organiser, marketer, planner, and so on. That is before we count all the hats we wear when we get home like mum, wife, supporter, provider. There are a lot. No wonder we are exhausted, snappy at home and losing the love for our business a lot of the time. I know I felt exactly that. I began to resent the business, working all hours and had no time to spend with my family and friends. In fact, what was the point of having the business? It was controlling me, and I was taking no money from the salon! It went through my head every day that I should just pack it all up, go bankrupt to get out of this hole of debt and work for someone else. As least I would get paid and have time off. It felt very appealing.

The problem is, coming back to juggling all those balls, we can't be good at everything; we can't do everything, and we all have the same number of hours in a day. I always say and think, as morbid as it is: If I was on my deathbed tomorrow... I wouldn't say, "I wish I worked more," I would more than likely say, "I wish I had spent more time with my family."

There is no point building a business if it isn't going to work for you and give you the freedom you wish for. To do this you need to learn to delegate. Hand over tasks to other members of your team or outsource jobs you don't like doing. I know handing over parts of your business to someone else is scary, but you can train someone to do exactly what you do, and in fact to do it even better than you do. With good training and practice when they are doing certain roles all day every day, they will no longer need you to help them or fix the problems they come across. Then that's a job ticked off your list that you no longer need to do.

I knew when I fell pregnant with Lola-Rose and then Brodee, that I wanted to be a present mum. I wanted to do the drop offs and pick-ups for school, even though after years of doing it, I can't wait to do them never again. I knew I wanted the school holidays off with them, even though I crave getting back to work after six weeks off. I wanted to make every school play and be able to pick them up if the school called to say they felt poorly. I have even pushed it further and homeschooled

Lola-Rose for nine months when she was having a tough time, while running three companies each turning over multiple six figures. The only way to do this was to let go of my inner control freak and let the team take over.

I had to learn the art of delegation which I would now say I am the queen of doing, after a lot of practises.

WHAT IS DELEGATION?

Delegation is giving tasks or responsibilities to others, mainly your team members, so that you can focus on higher-level tasks to carry on building the business. It means trusting your staff to handle certain aspects of the business, letting them take ownership and making sure the workload is done. When done right, delegation not only lightens your own load/to do list but boosts team morale by showing them that you have confidence in them and trust them. This leads to a more efficient, motivated and productive team. It also makes you a better employer because you are allowing your team to develop skills and have experiences that will make them better stylists or therapists. If you don't delegate, they might not grow to that next step in their career.

Let's break this down more and do a task together.

- Grab a pen and paper and note down everything you do day to day, both in your business and personally. It doesn't matter how big or small these tasks are, it's important you note every single one down. Track it each day if you need to, or after you do each task. When you pay attention to what you spend your time on, you will notice how much you really do. You might even discover you do lots of things you don't need to do or, most commonly, how much time you waste being unproductive.

- I generally advise tracking this for a week. Once a week is complete, analyse all the things you have done. What tasks did you really have to do yourself and what tasks could you have delegated to a team member or outsourced to a freelancer or professional. For example, if you spend time book-keeping, you could hire a book-keeper to free you up to do something else.

- Action this! Make sure you really do start to hand things over to others. If you want to grow, have freedom, and not have that to-do list forever, this is the first step to complete.

If you want a template of my opportunities list head over to: **www.kgbusinessmentor.com/book**

The problem I hear all the time is, "It will take me longer to show them how to do it, so I might as well do it myself," I understand completely that you are already time poor and it is quicker for you to just do it yourself rather than find more time to show someone else how to do that job. But no, this is the wrong thinking. You must think long term, not short term. In that moment, yes, of course it is quicker for you to do it. But once this person has learnt what to do, you will not need to do that task again. The more things you do this for, the more time you have.

Time is money. In our industry we exchange a service for money. So when we aren't carrying out a service, a lot of the time we think we can't make money. I always look at my tasks/jobs to do and now only do what I call 'money-making tasks'. These are the tasks I know are worth doing myself and will bring me more money straight away or will build up the business.

For example, social media posts or doing nails are not the correct things for me to do in the business. Yes, I used to do them both, but now I have a team in place for me to do higher money-making tasks like doing one-to-one business coaching calls or my business strategy for the year ahead. Think about what an hour of your time is worth to you. What is the maximum you can make per hour? Let's say it's £80 for a set of lashes in an hour: make sure you are mainly doing those treatments and your team are doing the lower ticket treatments. Then you are not withdrawing these treatments altogether, but the team are doing them instead as your time is worth more.

As the business grows, it will be more worth putting your time and energy into working on the business rather than in it. You will stop seeing an exchange in treatment time for money and instead look at the bigger picture, so you might stop doing treatments altogether like I did. I loved doing treatments and never thought I would stop. But when I retired from the tools at twenty-four years old, the business blew up with success as I was working *on* the business. I franchised the salon and had a chain across the country. I grew my coaching and product range, and my training to academies across the country. I couldn't have done any of this if I still offered treatments myself.

But before I stepped off the salon floor, before I became a business coach as my day to day, I was carrying out all the treatments, whether I loved them or not. It wasn't until I started to become unhappy doing everything that I knew something needed to change. I loved lashing, but I didn't really *love* doing the other treatments. I was great at doing them, and in the beginning, I needed to do it all to build the business. Once I won Eyelash Technician of the Year 2014, I became so busy with lashes that I got my chance to drop the other treatments and just do lashes, which at the time was all I wanted to do and was one of our biggest earning treatments in the salon alongside nail services. Lash treatments would take over £90,000 alone a year.

So, imagine when I offered solely lash services, which gave me more time to do to more clients, plus a price increase, alongside my team doing all the other treatments we offered, the money stacking effect came into play. We could take so much more money per hour with everyone doing treatments, me raising prices, and fitting more clients in, the income grew and grew, creating a stacking effect. Then take it a step further when I stepped away completely from treatments, added more team members and they took over the treatments and clients. We took half a million a year and I wasn't even doing treatments anymore. This is the beauty of having a team.

MINDSET SHIFT TO CEO

When we are hiring staff and growing the team, the hardest thing is getting our heads around our mindset and our potential employees'. The things I hear all the time are:

- Why would they work for me when they can work for themselves?
- I can't give them targets and let them know how much the business earns because they will leave.
- Why would they be motivated to work for me for a salary?
- How can I have time off and not supervise them?

I get that it is scary and that these questions have come into your mind. They entered mine too until I understood that my mindset as a business owner and theirs as employees are very different. As a business owner you put all this work in, most of the time for not a lot of money to begin with, but you know you are building your business. When someone comes to work for you, you wonder why they would want to work for someone else when they could do this on their own.

Not everyone *wants* to work for themselves. Not everyone thinks the same as those who build businesses. Lots of the questions above also come down to money blocks. As the business owner, you see the money that comes into the business and how much the business makes as a whole. Perhaps you feel guilty that the employee gets a wage which seems low compared to the treatment cost. What you are not factoring in are the business costs associated with that treatment and the time that treatment takes to do.

If it takes an hour to do a set of nails and it costs the client £40, that's not £40 profit, which an employee might think. Out of that £40 you need to deduct a staff member's wages, product costs and overall business costs. Whatever is left is profit. Unfortunately, this is very low in many cases… until the salon owner has worked with me. Sometimes there is no profit at all.

Instead of looking at the overall figure that the business turns over or your employee brings in, ask yourself what profit is left. Then you will not feel the guilt of paying your staff the going rate rather than the whole of that £40 per hour.

What about your employees' mindset, then? Why would they work for you when they could work for themselves? In short… not everyone wants their own business. Only around nine percent of people start a business (varying according to the economic conditions of different countries). Around twenty percent of small businesses fail within the first year and approximately fifty percent close within five years. By the ten-year mark only around thirty percent of businesses remain open.

Not everyone is business-minded like you. There are way more employee mindsets in the world than business mindsets. Most people want to know what money they will have at the end of the month: they want the security of knowing they are safe. So don't worry about that question, *Why would they work for me?* It is actually a huge positive that you are providing someone a job, helping someone put a roof over their heads and feed their children. Very few of us are risk-takers like you and me. Providing a job for someone is an incredible thing, so own it.

Lots of salon and clinic owners are scared to put targets in place for their teams. A lot of the time this comes down to you not having a CEO mindset. Of course you need to put targets in place. Even in corporate companies, employees have targets to hit.

You need to be sure of the following:

1. That your staff member is worth employing and brings you in money, otherwise what is the point? You don't build a team for fun, you build a team to earn more, grow the business and have more freedom. You need to know the break-even points your employee needs to bring in each month. That doesn't only mean their wages. After their wages you have to cover taxes, holiday pay and overheads. They need to bring in at least three or four times their wages for it to be worth having them in the business. This takes time and staff training, of course. Building up staff columns isn't an overnight thing – sometimes it takes six to twelve months for someone to get a full diary. However, it also takes you knowing your numbers. If you don't look into and implement targets for your staff, having them will cost you as a business.

2. That your staff stay motivated, and they know what is required of them. Human beings need goals to work towards. If you don't give someone targets, work becomes easy and unmotivating, which leads to boredom and them leaving. They need something to aim for. A team hitting their targets means they are working towards pay rises, team days out, training, new equipment and products. Now, instead of it looking like a target, it's more of a goal they can hit and can lead to a reward. There needs to be a benefit for the employee when they hit their target. This could take many forms, like £50 bonus if they bring in three times their wages, for example, or ten percent of the amount they went over their target. Set their targets according to how much money they are bringing into the business.

While targets can be motivating, you also need to look at other ways to keep your team happy and hardworking. Your motivation as the business owner will be different from theirs. Your motivation is more than likely money, freedom and not having to answer to anyone else. A lot of the time we assume our employees' motivation is money too, but it rarely is. Every person's motivation will be different and it is down to you as a boss and leader to find out what that is. What gets them up in the morning? What gives them the push to work and do a good job?

Let me give you some ideas of what can motivate a team member:

- Money. Of course, some people love money. Giving them cash bonuses, incentives and pay rises will keep them hungry to work harder.
- Praise. Some love praise, being told they have done well at a treatment or a task they have been given. Verbal praise, employee of the month or shout-outs in team meetings can go a long way.
- Training. Training incentives, promotion opportunities or doing an online programme might be a strong motivation for someone who loves learning. It gives them a buzz to push forward.
- Time off. Some people love their holidays and days off. An extra day off for hitting targets or doing well might be appreciated.
- Gifts. Others love a gift and appreciate a food voucher, candle or bottle of wine way more than £30 cash.

Everyone ticks differently and when you become a boss it's your job to find out each person's motivation. I suggest, however, that when employees hit their targets, you give them all the same monetary bonus in order to be fair across the team. But when they go the extra mile or hit other goals or targets you set them, you can reward them in the other ways above to keep them motivated.

DROP THE GUILT

I understand the guilt around having time off as a business owner or not physically working in the salon or clinic. But it needs to stop. To return to the stats I shared earlier, only nine percent of us are risk-takers enough to set up a business in the first place. If it was easy, everyone would do it. But it's not – far from it. Next time you want to go on holiday, take a day off or work from home rather than on reception, remember *you* took the risk to build this business. No one else. You have provided jobs because of this risk you took. You deserve that holiday or day off and you created a business so that you could work where you want to work.

In my salons, Saturday used to be the busiest day. Everyone was required to work without fail. If they couldn't work Saturdays, they wouldn't get the role. Also, the team could only take off four Saturdays a year. When I stopped doing treatments in the salon, I felt so guilty if I didn't go into the business and I felt even worse if I didn't work on a Saturday. At the time I had my daughter, Lola-Rose, every other weekend for a short amount of time. The weekends I didn't have her, I decided to go back to the salon and open up my diary on Saturdays only. This kept me occupied but I did it mainly because I felt guilty and thought I had no excuse not to work if I didn't have Lola-Rose with me. Before I knew it, I started working every Saturday, even on my weekends with Lola-Rose. I was in demand. Of course, I was in demand, I was the salon owner and people wanted me assuming I would be the best.

One Saturday when Lola-Rose was two, I had to take her to an appointment and I will always remember her saying, "Mummy, I have loved this weekend. I got to spend it with you." My heart broke. Why had I built up this chain of salons and started this brand, and had a child that's now in childcare a few days a week, if we were not spending weekends together? All because I was worried what my team would think of me if I was not there? Straight away I remembered why I stepped off the salon floor to begin with. I never went back to doing treatments again and I never felt guilty.

I also stopped justifying myself to other people. When I popped into the salon I always used to stress how busy I was, telling them everything I was doing when I wasn't in the salon because I didn't want them to think I was doing nothing. It became exhausting. I mean we all know there is always something to do as a business owner: it is impossible to do nothing!

We all know from the outside, people must think, "What is she doing if not treatments? Does she just go on holiday all the time?" They think, "She must have so much free time. She is so lucky." Sometimes clients came in when I was there and said, "Haven't seen you in so long. What are you doing in your free time now?" *Free time? Are you joking me?* One client even said to me once, "Oh, decided to work today, did you?" Honestly, the cheek of it.

You must put your CEO pants on. In the nicest way possible, your team don't care what you are doing. They are happy to have their jobs and just want to crack on. You know the work that comes with being a business owner. You know the risks you have taken; you know the sleepless nights you have had worrying about how to get more clients through the door or how to pay the wages this month. Everyone will have a different opinion. Let go of the self-doubt, guilt and justifying yourself to others and you will feel so much more free and become a better leader. I know I did.

In order to create a truly successful business, one that gives you the freedom you're working so hard for, you have to step fully into the role of a leader, a true CEO. Leadership isn't just about being in charge; it's about guiding your team, setting boundaries and creating an environment where everyone can grow, including you. It isn't just about the money; it's about building a company where people are motivated, valued and driven to help the business grow.

By being a fair leader, you set clear boundaries while being approachable and creating an environment where your team can come to you for guidance or support. Leadership also means knowing when to step back, trust your team and delegate tasks so you can focus on higher-level business decisions that will bring in more revenue and ultimately give you the freedom you want.

One of the hardest things for business owners, particularly in our industry, is learning to step away from daily operations. But if you want to scale, you have to. It is not enough to do the treatments and make the business tick day to day; you have to work on the business and spend time making it more profitable and expanding its impact. By empowering your team to take on responsibilities, you not only give yourself more time, you allow them to grow as professionals. Everyone benefits from this approach: your team feels trusted and valued and you free yourself to build your empire.

If you keep trying to control everything and don't delegate, you will hold back the potential growth of your business. The freedom you're chasing – the ability to take time off, travel and enjoy your life while your business continues to grow – comes from letting go. Trust your team, train them well and give them the tools to succeed so you can focus on being the CEO your business needs.

In the end, being a leader is about more than giving orders or delegating tasks, it's about creating a business that works for you and your team. Fairness, motivation and delegation are the key elements of success. When you lead with these values in mind, the entire team benefits. And when you learn to spend your time working *on* your business rather than *in* it, you'll finally be able to achieve the freedom and profitability you've always dreamed of.

So, ask yourself: Are you ready to step into the role of CEO, let go of the need for control, and allow your business, and your team, to go to the next level? The only thing standing between you and your dream of freedom is the ability to trust, delegate and lead.

9

HOW TO CREATE A FIVE-STAR BUSINESS

This concept brings your entire business together, making sure it's the go-to place and everyone raves about it. From the moment your clients find you to their experience inside your salon and even after they leave, every detail matters. I call this the customer journey, and it's one of the most important aspects of running a successful business.

Whether you're in the early stages of building your business, have just opened your doors, or have been established for a decade, I always say, "Put yourself in your client's shoes." What does their experience feel like from start to finish? Paying attention to detail in each step is what creates a five-star business that consistently gets five-star reviews and regular clientele. Let's walk through each step together to see where you can make changes within your business straight away.

STEP 1: VISIBILITY
– HOW EASY IS IT FOR CLIENTS TO FIND YOU?

It doesn't matter how incredible your services are if clients can't find you. Visibility is key, especially online. You need to be easily found on social media and search engines like Google, as well as in your local area. Most clients will find your business first through social media platforms like Instagram, Facebook or even TikTok. Your social media presence must be consistent, visually appealing and provide a clear idea of your services. Regular posting is a must. Sorry, I know it's an extra thing to do but it is non-negotiable. Show behind-the-scenes content, client transformations and even some personal stories about your journey as a business owner. Make sure your social media bios have direct links to your booking system or website. A London-based nail salon I worked with began posting daily on Instagram, showing their work, behind-the-scenes moments and client testimonials. After three months of consistent content, their follower count doubled and their booking rates increased by thirty percent.

Being visible on Google is just as important as your social media presence. When potential clients search for services like *hair salon near me* or *best beauty clinic in [your city],* you want your business to be at the top of those search results.

Optimise your 'Google My Business' profile with updated contact information, hours, photos and services offered. Encourage your regular clients to leave positive reviews, as this boosts your credibility and search ranking. A beauty clinic I had a strategy day with had no online presence beyond social media. After setting up and optimising their 'Google My Business' page, they saw an influx of new clients who found them through local searches. Their monthly revenue increased by twenty percent.

One of the most powerful tools for increasing visibility is leveraging local SEO. This includes optimising your website and online profiles to rank highly in local search results. When clients search for *nail salon near me* or *best brow specialist in [city]*, you want your business to be at the top.

Optimise your website with the right keywords, location tags and quality backlinks. If you haven't already, work with an SEO expert or use tools out there to help you with your content. A beauty therapist in Birmingham optimised her website for local search by including specific location keywords, like *Birmingham skin clinic* on every page. She also got happy clients to leave reviews, which improved her Google rankings, resulting in a fifteen percent increase in bookings within six months.

Understanding how social media algorithms work can significantly increase your visibility. The more engagement (likes, comments, shares) you get, the more often your content will appear in your audience's feed. Post consistently, and don't just focus on promoting services. Engage with your audience through polls, questions and interactive content like Instagram Stories or Reels. Using trending hashtags and geo-tags can also help improve discoverability. We use Instagram Stories to run polls about things like what nail art designs our clients prefer. We add stickers on nearly every story. This simple interaction boosts our engagement and helps us build and reach a larger audience, leading to being fully booked weeks in advance.

If you want to boost visibility quickly, investing in paid advertising like Facebook Ads or Google Ads can help. These platforms allow you to target potential clients based on location, age, interests and more, ensuring your promotions reach the right people.

Run a limited-time promotion (such as a discount on first-time visits) and target your local audience using paid ads. Be sure to track conversions so you know what works.

STEP 2: BOOKING
– HOW EASY IS IT FOR CLIENTS TO BOOK?

Once potential clients find you, the next step is making sure that booking an appointment is simple and seamless. If the process is confusing or unclear, you're likely losing out on clients every day.

Your booking links should be easily accessible and working. If clients struggle to find a way to schedule their appointments, they may move on to a competitor.

Include booking links clearly on your website, in your social media bios and in every post that promotes your services. If you use Instagram, there are tools that can help manage multiple links in one place.

In today's world, it's easy to overlook your phone ringing in the salon or clinic. However, some clients still prefer booking by phone and making sure that someone answers can make a huge difference in first impressions. I am very particular on this one thing. My team never let the phone ring out; it always needs to be answered as part of our policy, ideally within three rings. In the early days I would divert the salon phone to my mobile as I hated to miss an appointment on the days we were closed. I wouldn't recommend this now; you need a break to switch off, but I was desperate for every appointment. During your opening hours, though, I would make this non-negotiable. Have you ever tried to book dinner, just wanted to call up and book and no one answers the phone? It is frustrating as hell. When this happens to me, I end up booking elsewhere. So how many bookings are you missing out on?

Online booking is also now a must. There are no excuses not to have an online booking system. I hear all the time that people are worried it will book the wrong appointments or that they will have no control over it. This is rarely the case. Systems are so clever nowadays that it's smooth sailing when clients book in. If the worst comes to the worst and someone books at a time you don't want them to, just pick up the phone to change the appointment slightly. You will have heard the saying, 'Make money in your sleep.' If you have online bookings in place, this basically happens. Most clients book their appointments when your business is closed. You wake up to bookings being made 24/7 – it's great. Why would you want to turn these appointments away?

STEP 3: ARRIVAL
–WHAT'S THEIR FIRST IMPRESSION?

Your client's experience begins the moment they arrive at your salon or clinic, even before they walk in the door. Small details, like how easy it was to find, parking, whether the front of your business is tidy and inviting and how they are greeted set the tone for the entire visit.

Clients want an easy and stress-free experience from the moment they arrive. Consider how easy it is for them to park or to walk to your salon. Make parking and access information clear on your website and in booking confirmation emails. A client of mine who owns a salon in a busy city centre added parking instructions and even a Google Maps link to their booking confirmation emails. This simple step reduced late arrivals and improved the overall client experience.

Walking into a new environment can feel intimidating, especially for first-time clients. How they are greeted upon arrival plays a big role in how comfortable they feel. Do the team huddle around the reception area making it feel awkward when a client walks in? Maybe they are so busy there isn't anyone to give a warm welcome when they come through the door. Train your team to greet clients warmly, make eye contact and offer a welcome drink, like water, tea or coffee, especially if the client has arrived early for their appointment. In my salon, we have a whole refreshments menu for clients to choose a drink from and they love it.

The look, feel and cleanliness of your salon or clinic create an immediate impression. Every element can affect how your client feels when they walk in. Keep your reception area neat and consider how things like lighting, music and scent can enhance the space. Soft, warm lighting and subtle aromatherapy can help clients feel relaxed from the moment they step inside.

If you have a receptionist, this role is really important. They are the first point of human contact. Their warmth, smile, professionalism and ability to handle clients can either enhance or detract from the client experience.

If your business is difficult to access (e.g., no clear parking options or stairs-only entry), you risk alienating potential clients. Make sure your salon or clinic is easy to navigate, especially for clients with disabilities or mobility issues. Include clear parking and access instructions in your confirmation emails, and ensure your space is accessible to everyone. We added a handrail at the front of the salon as there is a small step and we also have access around the back for wheelchair access. Not only did this change open the salon to a new clientele, but it also demonstrated our commitment to inclusivity.

STEP 4: THE CONSULTATION PROCESS
– SETTING EXPECTATIONS

This step gets missed by so many, which I have never understood as it's the first thing we are taught in the industry. A thor-
ough consultation is essential for understanding your client's
needs, building rapport and setting clear expectations for the
service they are about to receive. Without a solid consultation,
you run the risk of not delivering what the client wants or
misunderstanding their needs. This step allows you to make
sure you and your client are on the same page before any
treatment begins. Spend extra time during the consultation to
ask detailed questions about what the client wants, their preferences and their expectations. Listen carefully and provide
professional advice if you think an alternative service might
be better suited to their needs.

A consultation is more than just asking what your client wants.
It is about building a relationship based on trust. Clients need to
feel heard, understood and valued from the very first conversation and this makes all the difference to their overall experience.

Use open-ended questions to understand the client's needs
fully. Pay attention not only to what they say but to their body
language. If a client seems unsure, offer professional advice or
suggestions to guide them toward the best decision. Remember
you're the professional and they trust you.

One of the biggest challenges in the beauty industry is setting
clear, realistic expectations. Clients sometimes come in with
Pinterest or Instagram photos, expecting to replicate those
results instantly. Be upfront about what is and isn't possible.
Use the consultation to manage expectations in terms of time,
results and cost, ensuring clients leave the appointment happy
with what you can realistically achieve.

If a client brings in photos of dramatic lash extensions that aren't suitable for their natural lashes, begin by explaining the potential risks during the consultation and showing the client alternative styles that would better suit their eyes. Clients appreciate the honesty and expertise, which will boost your referral rates.

STEP 5: THE TREATMENT
– IT'S SHOW TIME

By the time you begin the actual treatment, your client has already formed a strong opinion about your business. Now it's your time to shine.

The treatment itself is your opportunity to showcase your skills and expertise... but it's about more than just delivering a perfect service. You need to make the client feel valued and comfortable throughout the process. Engage with the client during the treatment but know when to let them relax in silence. Every client is different: some love to chat while others prefer a quiet experience. Learn to read the room.

We were one of the first salons to launch 'quiet time'. This is an option for clients to book a treatment and not be spoken to through the treatment other than the consultation process, with no questions asked. They can call up and request this or they can add a note to their online booking. This is great for clients who don't want that small talk chat or are going through something and just want some time out. Many clients really like having that option.

A five-star experience means paying attention to the small details that matter to each client. Whether it's remembering how many sugars they have in their tea or adjusting the room temperature, these little touches make a big difference. Use a client notes system to track individual preferences: this could include things like music choices, how they have their drink or sensitivity to certain products. This way, every treatment feels personal and customised to the client. A luxury spa I worked with made it a point to remember clients' favourite drinks and scents. If a client preferred a particular tea or essential oil, it was prepared before they arrived. This attention to detail made clients feel special and resulted in many five-star reviews mentioning these extras.

While delivering the treatment, your body language and communication skills matter just as much as the technical work itself. Being calm and confident in what you're doing helps the client feel relaxed and reassured.

STEP 6: AFTERCARE
– GOING THE EXTRA MILE

The treatment may be complete, but the experience doesn't end there. Aftercare is an essential part of ensuring clients get the best results and feel taken care of even after they leave your salon. Clear, detailed aftercare instructions show that you care about the long-term results of the service. Whether it's skincare tips, hair maintenance or product recommendations, aftercare is where you will stand out from your competitors.

Provide both verbal and written aftercare instructions. A small card with care guidelines or an email follow-up makes sure clients don't forget important details once they leave the salon. When clients leave your salon with clear instructions and product recommendations, it shows you care about their results beyond the treatment. This builds trust and encourages long-term loyalty. Always ask clients if they have any questions about aftercare and let them know they can follow up if they experience any issues or have concerns. Always remember this with your regular clients too. Sometimes when we see our regular clients we don't give them aftercare as we assume they know. They might have forgotten or need a reminder, but above all, it makes you look more professional rather than slacking because they have had this treatment before with you.

STEP 7: RETAIL
– SELLING WITHOUT FEELING SALESY

So many beauty professionals are uncomfortable with the idea of selling, but retailing products that complement your treatments is an essential part of a five-star experience. It does not mean being pushy but offering clients something that will help them maintain their results. If you've provided a treatment that requires maintenance or aftercare, failing to recommend the right products is doing your clients a disservice. Retailing is an extension of the care you're providing. During the treatment or consultation, explain why certain products would benefit the client and help prolong the results of their treatment. Frame retailing as part of the service, rather than as an extra sales push. When done correctly, clients will appreciate your recommendations and trust your expertise. If you don't sell it to them, someone else will or they will get something from the supermarket they think they should which could reverse what you have done. Retail sales can also increase your takings by twenty to forty percent. Why would you not want to earn that extra income for doing nothing other than advising?

When you think of retail as problem-solving, it becomes less intimidating. If a client has just had a keratin treatment, they need sulphate-free shampoo to maintain the results. If they've had a facial, they need to follow a proper skincare regimen to sustain the glow. You're not just selling a product; you're offering a solution that benefits your clients in the long run. If you do not do this, you are doing your client a disservice.

If you're serious about retailing, which you should be, consider creating a designated space in your salon or clinic for products. This space should feel inviting rather than locking away products, so clients can browse, touch and ask questions without pressure. Clients are more likely to buy products when they understand how those products will benefit them. This is where education becomes an important part of the retail process. Rather than just telling clients what to buy, explain why they need it and how it will work for them. If you have a team, make sure they have tried the products themselves and understand the benefits. We can't sell anything that we don't believe in.

STEP 8: TAKING PAYMENT AND REBOOKING – DON'T LET THE EXPERIENCE END TOO SOON

Just because the treatment is over, it doesn't mean the client experience is. How you handle the final interaction, taking payment, offering aftercare advice, and encouraging a rebooking, can really make a difference. These small, final details are what make a five-star business stand out.

Clients don't want awkwardness when it's time to pay. Your team should feel confident handling money and your payment system should be quick, efficient and professional. Make sure your team is well-trained in all payment systems, including Apple Pay, and able to answer any questions about pricing or promotions. If you offer high-ticket treatments you can even have payment plan options to make it easier for clients to buy into these treatments.

Rebooking should be part of your regular client flow. Asking clients to schedule their next appointment ensures they stay loyal to your business and don't look elsewhere. Plus, it's easier to secure repeat business than to attract new clients.

After taking payment, always ask, "Shall we get your next few appointments in now, Sally? I know you like six o'clock on a Wednesday and I don't want that space to go for you."

It is so important these rebookings are done to get a fully booked diary in advance, which is what we all wish for. If you don't do this, yes, they can book online. But we all know how busy life gets and before you know it, they have forgotten to get their appointment and now it's an appointment dragged out. The secret to a fully booked diary is getting them booked in before they leave.

Even as your client is leaving, the customer journey isn't quite over. How they feel walking out the door matters. Whether it's a friendly goodbye, a reminder about their aftercare or an offer of further support, this final step solidifies the experience.

Train your team to always thank clients for coming, offer any necessary aftercare advice one more time, and invite them to follow up if they have any questions about their treatment. A beauty clinic I worked with started offering a complementary product sample with every appointment, which kept clients thinking about the clinic long after their appointment. It made them feel valued and increased repeat visits. We also give welcome bags to all new clients which helps them return as they all get a £5 voucher on their second visit to the salon and some branded goodies so they remember us. Have a think about different ways you can add to your business to get them returning.

GOING BEYOND THE APPOINTMENT: BUILDING LONG-TERM RELATIONSHIPS

One part of building a five-star business is the ability to grow long-term relationships with your clients. This doesn't happen by accident. It requires strategic follow-up, consistent engagement and genuine care for your clients.

Don't let the client experience end when they walk out the door. Sending follow-up emails or messages after an appointment keeps you in the client's mind and makes them feel valued. Send a personalised thank-you message within twenty-four hours of the appointment and follow up with a reminder about aftercare or any products you recommend. This can normally be done through whatever booking system you use.

LOYALTY PROGRAMMES

Implementing a loyalty programme is a great way to keep clients coming back. Rewarding clients for repeat visits or referrals creates a sense of loyalty and encourages them to continue choosing your business over others.

There are different loyalty systems you can put in place that suit your business. The most common one is stamps. A client comes in and receives a stamp on every visit. The fifth time and the tenth time they get a reward. That could be anything from a free treatment, a percentage off or a discount on another service. In my salon, we have a point system which I love. £1 spent gives them one point. The points build up and equate to free treatments. The more points they save, the more valuable the treatments are available. What I love the most... they can only choose a treatment they haven't had before in the salon. This gives the client an opportunity to try something for free that they might not have booked in for before.

Yes, it's a free treatment but you have to look at the bigger picture. If that client loves the treatment, how much extra will that client now spend with you every month? What is that client now worth to you a year? You will see that it's a lot more than giving away the free treatment. This is a great way to raise a client's average spend. If you have a loyalty system where the client gets money off the treatment they always have, you're giving away money for nothing. They were going to come back for that treatment regardless of the £5 off on the tenth visit.

Referral systems are always great to have in place too. So many businesses don't offer them. Those that do, I hear they don't work. There are a few reasons why a referral system doesn't work:

It's not advertised anywhere that you even offer a system.

How can it work if it's a secret? You need to let clients know that you offer a referral system. Have little cards to pop them on the reception desk for them to take. Put them along the nail bars to spark conversation or get your team to give them out. You can also advertise that you have a referral system on your socials and emails. You could even take it one step further and give shout-outs on social media to clients who have recommended someone, giving them the spotlight. If you tag them, hopefully they will re-share and that will help you gain more new followers and clients. Creating a buzz will get others to want to rave about your business too for the recognition.

The client who refers doesn't get anything.

Offering a referral system that doesn't give the existing client anything rarely works. Did you know that if someone has a bad experience in your business, they tell on average twenty people about that experience and how unhappy they are. Awful,

I know. If a client has a good experience, they are likely to tell fewer than three people. This proves that you need to give something to the client as an incentive for them to share and it must be good. I recommend giving the existing client more than the new client. Why? Because they have done the work for you and gaining new clients all the time can be expensive. So, see this as good marketing spend. In my salon, we give out have referral cards. The client gets £10 off their next treatment once a new client has been in and the new client gets £5 off. Everyone is happy.

ONGOING MARKETING

After your client has been in, had the best experience with you and had the follow-up emails within twenty-four hours, you need to carry on engaging with the client through your marketing tactics. Regular email marketing, social media engagement and personal reach out are so important, helping you stand out and make sure a competitor doesn't shine above you. If you performed an amazing five-star service and you did all the above, but for some reason the client wasn't able to rebook at the time, as their life gets busy, so does their scrolling on social media and their inbox with other salons' content feeding and tempting their minds to book in with them. This is why consistency is key, always showing up and marketing, so you are at the forefront of clients' minds all the time.

Creating a five-star business is about much more than delivering great treatments. You need to understand every touchpoint in the customer journey, from the moment they find you online to walking out the door. By mastering each step: visibility, booking, client interaction, aftercare, retail and follow-up, you not only create an exceptional client experience but build a strong business that clients want to return to and recommend to others. As you grow, always keep the client journey in mind. Put yourself in the client's shoes for a day and see what would you change within your business. Go through the steps with your team if you have one and see what ideas they come up with to enhance each step to be better than it already is. A five-star business isn't just about the treatment, it's about how you make your clients feel throughout every single step. When your clients leave not only looking great but feeling valued and cared for, you know you've truly built something extraordinary.

10

THE LAST STRETCH

Congratulations! You have made it to the end of this book and that alone is a massive achievement. You have taken the time to invest in yourself and your business, and for that, I'm so excited for you. If there are chapters you haven't read because you don't think you need them yet, I encourage you to return to them as soon as you've taken action on the chapters you have read. Reading about every area of growing your business will help you create the success and freedom you really desire.

You have an exciting journey ahead of you and I can't wait to see the growth you'll achieve. There's so much more I wanted to cover in this book, but I'd need several volumes to include everything, for example, topics like traditional branding, creating multi sites or franchises, growing an academy, starting your own product range and PR could each have its own book. They're all aspects of scaling your business and I want you to know that I cover these in-depth in my programmes and masterminds. I see businesses really take off when they develop in these areas.

I look forward to helping you explore them if you choose to dive deeper into this journey with me.

I hope you've seen that my journey wasn't easy and that success wasn't handed to me on a plate. There were plenty of struggles, setbacks and doubts along the way. I want you to take from this the message that putting in the work and staying committed to your vision pays off. I hope my experiences and the lessons I've shared have shown you that the rewards, both financial and those of personal freedom, are absolutely worth it.

When I started my salon, I had no idea where it would lead. I had a passion for the beauty industry and a desire to create something of my own, but I couldn't have imagined the level of success and freedom I've experienced today. If I hadn't taken that risk, if I hadn't started my salon, I wouldn't have the businesses, the brand or the opportunities I have now.

But just as important as starting the salon was the moment I decided to step *out* of the salon. I knew that if I stayed behind the chair, on the tools, my growth would always be limited. It wasn't easy to let go at first. I was used to doing everything myself, having control and being the main earner, the one all the clients wanted. But I knew that for my business to grow, I needed a team. Putting down the tools and stepping into a leadership role was one of the best decisions I ever made. Without doing that, I would never have had the chance to travel the world with my children, have my multiple businesses or experience the freedom I have now.

I have tried to be as open as possible in this book because I know how much it would have helped me to have this kind of guidance when I was starting out. I hope my stories – the good, the bad and everything in between – have shown you that you can create the business you want, the way you want. I hope you've learned valuable strategies, picked up tips that will help you avoid common mistakes and gained the confidence to take your business to the next level.

If you only take away one thing from this, I hope it's that you have the power to create the business and life you dream of. There will be challenges along the way, but if you keep showing up, keep working on your goals and stay focused on why you started, you can make it happen.

Always remember why you started this business in the first place. There will be times when things get tough and you'll be tempted to go off track. It is easy to get caught up in what other people are doing or what you think you 'should' be doing because social media tells you to or because those around you are following a certain path. But don't lose sight of your own vision.

Stay true to yourself. Do what makes you happy and aligns with your purpose. Don't feel pressured to follow trends or do what everyone else is doing. Your journey is unique and the only person who knows what's best for your business is you. Build your business in a way that not only brings you success but also brings you joy. This is your journey and it's important to enjoy the process as much as the outcome.

This is the end of this book but not the end of your journey: it's only the beginning. You have all the tools and knowledge you need to start making changes in your business today. Whether it's refining your client experience, improving your marketing or building a stronger team, the next steps are in your hands.

And if you want to take things even further, there's always more to explore. As I mentioned earlier, topics like branding, franchising, becoming a product owner and PR are parts of the puzzle that we didn't get to dive into here. These areas can transform your business and take it to a whole new level, and

I cover them in detail in my programmes and masterminds. If you're ready to go deeper and explore these topics with me, and even deeper on topics like marketing and teams, I'd love to continue helping you on your journey. I would love for you to connect with me on **www.instagram.com/kg_katiegodfrey** as that's where I hang out the most and you can download your free book resources over at **www.kgbusinessmentor.com/book**

As you close this book, take a moment to feel proud of yourself for making it this far. You have committed to growing your business, and that's worth celebrating. I'm so excited for you and can't wait to see the incredible things you're going to achieve.

Remember, success isn't just about the destination, it's about the journey. Keep learning, keep growing and keep pushing yourself to be the best version of you and your business. With the right mindset, the right strategies and the determination to keep going, there's no limit to what you can achieve.

Thank you for allowing me to be a part of your journey. I can't wait to see where it takes you next!

Grow, believe, achieve. Lots of love and success,

Katie Godfrey

ABOUT THE AUTHOR

Katie Godfrey is a salon owner, educator, product owner and business strategist who went from being £50,000 in debt to building a globally recognised beauty empire. At just 19, she opened her first salon, learning invaluable lessons about marketing, leadership, and resilience along the way. Today, Katie mentors beauty, hair, and aesthetics entrepreneurs world-wide, helping them step off the salon floor, gain financial freedom, and build businesses they truly love.

As the founder of multiple salons, training academies, and a product range, she understands first-hand the challenges of juggling many roles. Through her writing and coaching, Katie shares honest insights, proven systems, and the mindset shifts that made her success possible, empowering others to do the same.

CONTACT

www.instagram.com/kg_katiegodfrey

www.facebook.com/katiegodfreybusinessmentor

www.linkedin.com/in/katie-godfrey-882284123

www.kgbusinessmentor.com/book